高职基础英语Ⅲ(上)

主 编 邹 霞 孙 晶 赖铭艳 李慎明
副主编 朱水连 吴婷婷 范 静

哈尔滨工业大学出版社

内容简介

本教材共有5个单元,每个单元都有独立的主题,分别是 Freshman、Traditional Festival、Internet、Travel 和 Economy。单元的设计和编排充分考虑题材和难易度,每个单元采用模块化设计,包括 Listening、Spotlight on Reading、Building up More Skills 和 Leisure Time 四个模块,从听、说、读、写、译等方面进行针对性的教学和训练。

本教材适用于非英语专业的高职学生。

图书在版编目(CIP)数据

高职基础英语:Ⅲ.上/邹霞等主编. —哈尔滨:
哈尔滨工业大学出版社,2023.6(2024.8 重印)
ISBN 978-7-5767-0938-4

Ⅰ.①高… Ⅱ.①邹… Ⅲ.①英语-高等职业教育-教材 Ⅳ.①H319.39

中国国家版本馆 CIP 数据核字(2023)第138140号

策划编辑	杨秀华 薛 力
责任编辑	陈 洁
出版发行	哈尔滨工业大学出版社
社 址	哈尔滨市南岗区复华四道街10号 邮编150006
传 真	0451-86414749
网 址	http://hitpress.hit.edu.cn
印 刷	哈尔滨市工大节能印刷厂
开 本	787mm×1092mm 1/16 印张7.25 字数172千字
版 次	2023年6月第1版 2024年8月第2次印刷
书 号	ISBN 978-7-5767-0938-4
定 价	42.00元

(如因印装质量问题影响阅读,我社负责调换)

序

《国家职业教育改革实施方案》指出:"职业教育与普通教育是两种不同教育类型,具有同等重要地位。改革开放以来,职业教育为我国经济社会发展提供了有力的人才和智力支撑,现代职业教育体系框架全面建成,服务经济社会发展能力和社会吸引力不断增强,具备了基本实现现代化的诸多有利条件和良好工作基础。"职业教育在向制造业和服务业培养和输送高技能人才方面起到了积极的作用。我国中学后教育一般分为中专、大专、本科及研究生四个教育层次。随着对教育和实践的不断探索与改革,渐渐地分成两类四个层次,即职业教育类和普通教育类。以前的中专和大专蜕变而成时下的职业中专和高职,而本科、研究生则新增了职业本科和专业硕、博研究生。通常,高职又分为初中起点的五年一贯制高职与高中起点的三年制高职(大专)。时下,职业中专与三年制高职的基础文化教材相对较为成熟,而五年一贯制高职通常实施的培养方案是"3+2"学年模式。在"实习"与"就业市场化"的双重因素作用下,这种模式中的"2"既不能较好地学专业,也不能达到大专本应有的再学习所具备的基础理论的教学要求。这种教学模式使用的教材多半是中职教材+大专教材,不成体系,这种加法或因内容重叠而与课时不匹配,或因课时所限致使讲授的内容难以服务后续专业课程的学习;难以实现夯实基础文化和奠定终身发展的基础教育的教学目的。为此,我院教授聂高辉博士组织公共课教学部语文、数学、英语三个教研室从事职业教育多年的有经验的教师积极开展教学研究并取得一系列研究成果,基于这些研究成果编写了适合我院职业教育改革与创新的职业教育基础文化系列教材。

我院的职业教育改革是以基础理论为基,以技术技能为本,践行习近平总书记关于职业教育工作的重要指示"培养更多高素质技术技能人才、能工巧匠、大国工匠"。

这套职业教育基础文化系列教材既具有"课程思政"元素,又具有来自于具体行业的应用案例。教材的内容选取和安排既符合《职业院校教材管理办法》文件要求,又与我校各专业培养方案相匹配。同时,教材还具有随学校深度改革和高质量发展的动态要求而扩展的空间。我院公共课教学部教师在繁重的教学任务下还能不断创新职业教育,探索职业教育文化基础教育的规律和方法,实属难能可贵。

我院逐渐形成了遵循学生的个性特点实施教育培养的传统,让具有不同兴趣和基础的学生都能够学有所长。用创新精神编写教材,让进入我院学习的各类特长学生拥有扎实的文化基础和创新精神。希望这一系列教材的出版有益于我院"学历+学力"的职教育人模式的探索,为促进我院高质量发展发挥应有的作用。

江西洪州职业学院院长

2023 年 6 月

前　言

五年制高职英语教材共分《高职基础英语Ⅰ》《高职基础英语Ⅱ》《高职基础英语Ⅲ》，每一本都由上下两册构成。《高职基础英语Ⅲ》（上、下册）各由10个话题构成，每个话题都是一个独立的单元。每个单元中心突出，环环相扣，层层展开。编写由浅入深，循序渐进，符合英语学习的认知规律，符合《高等职业教育专科英语课程标准》要求。

本教材包括5个单元，每个单元采用模块化设计，共包括 **Listening**、**Spotlight on Reading**、**Building up More Skills** 和 **Leisure Time** 4个基本模块。单元的设计和编排既考虑到题材和难易度，也照顾到策略训练的先后顺序，从而有针对性地帮助学生应对大学英语三级B级考试。

Listening 为听力练习，以长短对话和短文填空的方式呈现，旨在激发学生的学习兴趣，引导学生主动参与到课堂学习中，充分锻炼其听力能力。

Spotlight on Reading 包括精读和泛读两个部分，每部分内容均包含一篇文章和相关练习，旨在帮助学生掌握丰富的文化知识和提高阅读能力。

Building up More Skills 包括语法和应用文写作两个部分，其中 Grammar Tips 部分，主要对英语的时态、非谓语动词、宾语从句和定语从句等进行概括性的复习，理论阐述以够用为度，注重实训练习。为学生梳理重要的语法知识，旨在帮助学生掌握重点语法知识。Practical Writing 则系统地介绍了 Letter、E-mail、Application 和 Resume 等应用文的写作方法，提供了范文和模拟写作练习，旨在指导学生将各单元所学的知识融会贯通，并将其运用到写作训练中，让学生掌握日常生活和工作中常用的应用文写作。

Leisure Time 特意设计了影视、流行的英文歌曲欣赏以及趣味英语知识，旨在寓教于乐地提高学生文化素养，从多角度为学生的语言学习营造生动多元的文化氛围和丰富多彩的语言环境，从而使语言学习、应用以及文化体验相结合。

本教材由邹霞、孙晶、赖铭艳、李慎明任主编，其中，邹霞负责教材编写大纲的制定及各单元内容的衔接，并参与编写 Unit 1、Unit 2、Unit 3、Vocabulary Index 以及 Irregular Verbs 等部分；由朱水连、吴婷婷和范静任副主编。

尽管编者们具有丰富的高职教学经验，但因水平有限，书中难免存在不完善和疏漏之处，敬请广大读者给予指正。

在编写本教材的过程中,我们借鉴了英语应用能力 B 级考试真题及部分网络资源,在此向这些材料的作者表示最诚挚的谢意。此外,还要感谢学校各级领导对本教材出版的大力支持。

编　者

2022 年 11 月

目　　录

Unit 1　Freshman ··· 1
　　Module Ⅰ　Listening ·· 3
　　Module Ⅱ　Spotlight on Reading ································· 4
　　Module Ⅲ　Building up More Skills ···························· 12
　　Module Ⅳ　Leisure Time ·· 17

Unit 2　Traditional Festival ·· 19
　　Module Ⅰ　Listening ·· 21
　　Module Ⅱ　Spotlight on Reading ······························· 22
　　Module Ⅲ　Building up More Skills ···························· 29
　　Module Ⅳ　Leisure Time ·· 36

Unit 3　Internet ··· 39
　　Module Ⅰ　Listening ·· 41
　　Module Ⅱ　Spotlight on Reading ······························· 42
　　Module Ⅲ　Building up More Skills ···························· 51
　　Module Ⅳ　Leisure Time ·· 56

Unit 4　Travel ·· 59
　　Module Ⅰ　Listening ·· 61
　　Module Ⅱ　Spotlight on Reading ······························· 62
　　Module Ⅲ　Building up More Skills ···························· 69
　　Module Ⅳ　Leisure Time ·· 74

Unit 5　Economy ··· 77
　　Module Ⅰ　Listening ·· 79
　　Module Ⅱ　Spotlight on Reading ······························· 80
　　Module Ⅲ　Building up More Skills ···························· 87
　　Module Ⅳ　Leisure Time ·· 92

Appendix A　Vocabulary Index ··· 94

Appendix B　Irregular Verbs ··· 101

References ·· 106

UNIT 1

Freshman

Unit 1 Freshman

Learning Objectives

Students should be able to
★ Understand the dialogues and passages by listening.
★ Be familiar with the college life and talk about it.
★ Master the new words and expressions.
★ Review the usage of Tense.
★ Master the format of letter and learn to write.

Module Ⅰ Listening

Task 1 Listen to the following conversations twice and choose the best answer to each question you hear in the recording.

1. A. From her friend.   B. From her teacher.
   C. From her boss.   D. From her brother.
2. A. Attend a meeting.   B. Hold a party.
   C. Take an interview.   D. Meet a friend.
3. A. In the meeting room.   B. In her office.
   C. At home.   D. At the bank.
4. A. It's very boring.   B. That's too busy.
   C. He likes it very much.   D. He's going to give it up.
5. A. An engineer.   B. A doctor.
   C. A salesman.   D. A secretary.

Task 2 Listen to the following passage twice and fill in the blanks with the missing words you hear in the recording.

People visit other countries for many reasons. Some travel __6__; others travel to visit interesting places. Whenever you go, for whatever reason, it is important to be __7__. A tourist can draw a lot of attention from local people. Although most of the people you meet are friendly and welcoming, sometimes there are dangers. __8__, your money or passport might be stolen. Just as in your home country, do not expect everyone you meet to be friendly and __9__. It is important to prepare your trip in advance, and __10__ be careful while you are traveling.

Module Ⅱ Spotlight on Reading

Text A Intensive Reading

Tips for Freshmen's Success

1   Every freshman **steps** on campus with the **aim** of success in mind. If you are a new college student, the following tips can help you **achieve** a good start this term. Remember that school is important, as is the knowledge you take away from it, so take your **education seriously** and you will succeed.

About Study Tips

2   Study with friends. Your friends may see new ways to solve problems, and they might be easier to understand than your teachers.

3   Learn from **failure**. Nobody can **excel** in everything all of the time. Don't be so hard on yourself and try to learn from mistakes and move on.

4   Don't miss your class. If you don't go to class, you may miss **valuable** information that can only be found in the classroom. Not going to class will also tell the teacher that you are not serious about your education.

About **Stress Reduction**

5   Use lists. Making to-do lists can help you **organize** what needs to be done. When you finish something, cross it off the list.

6   **Treat** yourself right. If you are sleepy, go to sleep. If you are hungry, eat. Listen to your body when it is telling you something.

7   Don't be **afraid** to have fun. After you have had a long day of study, you need some fun to help reduce the stress. Enjoy your fun time and don't bring your work into it.

Unit 1 Freshman

New Words

tip	/tɪp/	n. 诀窍,建议
success	/sək'ses/	n. 成功,胜利
step	/step/	v. 跨步走;踏 n. 迈步
aim	/eɪm/	n. 目标,目的
achieve	/ə'tʃiːv/	v. 获得,完成,达到
education	/ˌedʒu'keɪʃ(ə)n/	n. 教育
seriously	/'sɪərɪəsli/	adv. 严肃地,认真地
failure	/'feɪljə(r)/	n. 失败;失败的人
excel	/ɪk'sel/	v. 精通,擅长
valuable	/'væljuəb(ə)l/	adj. 贵重的;有益的
stress	/stres/	n. 精神压力,紧张
reduction	/rɪ'dʌkʃ(ə)n/	n. 减小,降低
organize	/'ɔːgənaɪz/	v. 组织
treat	/triːt/	v. 对待,看待
afraid	/ə'freɪd/	adj. 害怕的;担心的

Phrases and Expressions

take away 带走;拿走
be hard on 对……苛刻;对……要求严格
move on 往前走,前进
cross off 从……划掉,删除
bring into 使开始;使进入某种状态

Inquiry Learning

1. **Remember that school is important, as is the knowledge you take away from it...**
   记住,学校跟你从其中获得的知识一样重要……
   句中 as 是连接词,引导非限制性定语从句,指代上文提及的整个句子,表示其后的人或事情跟上文所述的某人或某事相同。从理解的角度讲,"as is the knowledge you take away from it" 等于 "the knowledge you take away from it is also important"。"you take away from it" 是定语从句,修饰 knowledge。

2. **Not going to class will also tell the teacher that you are not serious about your education.**
   不去上课也会告诉老师你对自己的教育不认真。
   句首的动名词短语 Not going to class 是全句的主语。课文中类似的句子还有:"Making to-do lists can help you organize what needs to be done."。
   如:Seeing is believing. 眼见为实。

3. **Making to-do lists can help you organize what needs to be done.**
   列出待办事项清单可以帮你有条理地处理需要做的事情。
   to-do lists 待办事项清单。

4. **Listen to your body when it is telling you something.**
   注意听取身体的诉求。
   句中 listen to 可解释为"注意,留意"。when 后的代词 it 指上文中的"身体",tell you something 可解释为"告诉你它的状况或需求"。

Reading Comprehension

Choose the best answer according to the passage.

1. The author suggests studying with friends because _____ .
   A. it is sometimes easier to understand them than your teachers
   B. they sometimes know more than your teachers
   C. it makes you feel happier to solve problems with others
   D. they take their education seriously and are successful

2. If you miss your class, your teacher will know that _____ .
   A. you never learn from mistakes
   B. you don't have any friends in class
   C. you can get valuable information from other people
   D. you don't take your education seriously

3. A "to-do list" is a list of things that _____ .
   A. have been done

Unit 1 Freshman

  B. need to be done

  C. you don't want to do

  D. you love to do

4. "Listen to your body when it is telling you something" means that _____.

  A. you should listen to other people when they are talking to you

  B. you should take care of yourself because no one else can do it for you

  C. if you feel tired, you should listen to some music

  D. if you feel tired, you should take a break

5. Talking about having fun, the author doesn't think it a good idea _____.

  A. to take a five or ten minutes' break while working under stress

  B. to have a long day of study

  C. to keep your work in mind while you go out to enjoy your fun

  D. to go to sleep during the day

Language in Use

Task 1 Find the right definition in column B that matches the words in column A.

Column A	Column B
1. achieve	A. in a way that shows that you think sth. is important
2. education	B. an act of making sth. less or smaller
3. seriously	C. lack of success
4. failure	D. succeed in doing sth.
5. reduction	E. the process of teaching and learning
6. stress	F. pressure or worry caused by the problems in sb.'s life

Task 2 Fill in the blanks with the given words or expressions. Change the form where necessary.

excel	tip	allow	be hard on	cross off	reduction

1. Listening to music is a good way to _____ stress.
2. Jane is a professional teacher of education and she can give your son a few _____ on how to study in college.
3. John can speak English and French. He has always _____ at foreign languages.
4. Most successful students _____ themselves, but my classmate Mark is different.
5. I usually write down everything before go shopping. When we have bought something, we _____ it _____ the list.
6. This DVD _____ you to record TV programs and watch them later.

Translation

Task 1 Translate the following sentences from Chinese into English with the phrases given in the brackets.

1. 他小时候擅长音乐和美术。(excel)

   _____

2. 此书就近来的发展趋势提供了宝贵的信息。(valuable)

   _____

3. 要达到这些目标需要齐心协力。(achieve)

   _____

4. 划掉那些最不会在你身上发生的选项。(cross off)

   _____

5. 把这些玻璃杯和托盘拿走。(take away)

   _____

Task 2 Translate the following sentences from English into Chinese.

1. There has been some reduction in unemployment.

   _____

2. They recognized the need to take the problem seriously.

   _____

3. We ought to organize more social events.

   _____

4. We will work to get this law approved and bring into effect.

   _____

5. I think he didn't mean to be hard on you.

   _____

Text B   Extensive Reading

The Advantages of Learning English

1   There are one **billion** people in this world who are just like you. One billion people trying to understand the difference between much and many. One billion people trying to **pronounce** TH and make it sound **natural**. There are one billion people trying to learn English. This is because English has become the most important language in the world.

2   As the world becomes smaller there will soon be no way to **avoid** English. So why not learn it now? Look at all the advantages you can have...

   Access to Knowledge and Information

3   Most of the web pages on the Internet are in English. The Internet has a huge amount of

information, some of which can only be accessed in English. English will **allow** you to **chat** with people from all over the world in email, games and other services.

Advancing Your Career

4　If you are interested in **advancing** in the business world, English is a key to success. Most countries in some way will do business with English-speaking countries. English has also become the **international** language of business and is often used as a **neutral** language for business between **various** countries.

Entertainment

5　You will **be able to** read books written by American, British, and other English-speaking authors without needing the **translated copy**.

6　Learning English will allow you to watch movies in their **original** language. When you learn English you can finally understand what your favorite song on the radio is saying.

7　Learning English will give you the **ability** to travel to English-speaking countries like the United States, Canada, England, and Australia. English is spoken in more than 100 countries and is often the only way to **communicate** in a foreign country.

New Words

advantage	/əd'vɑːntɪdʒ/	n. 有利条件,优势
billion	/'bɪljən/	num. 10亿
pronounce	/prə'naʊns/	v. 发(音),读(音)
natural	/'nætʃ(ə)rəl/	adj. 天然的

avoid	/əˈvɔɪd/	v.	避免，防止
access	/ˈækses/	n.	入口　v. 接近
allow	/əˈlaʊ/	v.	允许，准许
chat	/tʃæt/	v.	闲聊
service	/ˈsɜːvɪs/	n.	服务
advance	/ədˈvɑːns/	v.	（使）前进；发展
international	/ˌɪntəˈnæʃ(ə)nəl/	adj.	国际的
neutral	/ˈnjuːtrəl/	adj.	中立的
various	/ˈveərɪəs/	adj.	各种各样的
entertainment	/ˌentəˈteɪnmənt/	n.	娱乐
translate	/trænzˈleɪt/	v.	翻译
copy	/ˈkɒpi/	n.	复印件，副本
original	/əˈrɪdʒən(ə)l/	adj.	起初的，原先的
ability	/əˈbɪləti/	n.	能力
communicate	/kəˈmjuːnɪkeɪt/	v.	交流，传递信息

Phrases and Expressions

a huge amount of 大量的
try to do 尝试做某事
why not 为什么不
be interested in... 对……感兴趣
be able to 能够

Inquiry Learning

1. **One billion people trying to learn... One billion people trying to understand... One billion people trying to pronounce...** 10亿人在努力学习……，10亿人在努力理解……，10亿人在努力发……音。
   这是一个名词词组的排比结构，重点强调one billion people，trying to 引导的分词短语修饰one billion people。

2. **As the world becomes smaller there will soon be no way to avoid English.** 随着世界一点点变小，很快将无法避开英语。
   as 用作连词时，可以用来表示时间，译为"正当……的时候；随着……；边……边……"，引导时间状语从句。与when、while相比，as 多用于口语，强调"同一时间""时间一先一后""随着"。

如:As I was going out, it began to rain. 当我出门时,开始下雨了。

As time goes on, he will understand what I said. 随着时间的推移,他会理解我所讲的话。

3. **The internet has a huge amount of information, some of which can only be accessed in English.** 互联网有大量的信息,其中有些只能用英语获取。

some of which 引导一个非限制性定语从句,与主句相连。用这样的结构可以把两个简单句合成一个主从复合句。

如:She bought a dozen eggs yesterday.

Many of the eggs were broken when she arrived home.

→ She bought a dozen eggs yesterday, many of which were broken when she arrived home.

4. **English has also become the international language of business and is often used as a neutral language for business between various countries.** 英语也已成为国际商务用语,在不同的国家之间谈生意时常被用作中立语言。

neutral 原指"中性的,中立的",此处的意思是不同国家"共同使用的",因此,a neutral language 也可理解为"中介语言"。

5. **When you learn English you can finally understand what your favorite song on the radio is saying.** 学了英语你就终于能理解电台上你最喜欢的歌唱的是什么了。

"what your favorite song on the radio is saying"是 understand 的宾语从句,相当于"the things that your favorite song on the radio is saying"。

Reading Comprehension

Choose the best answer according to the passage.

1. How are the one billion people just like you? _____

    A. We all live on earth.

    B. We are all learning English.

    C. We all speak several languages.

    D. We all love English movies.

2. English is sometimes necessary when you use the Internet because _____.

    A. some information can only be found in English

    B. you need to use English in the chat-rooms

    C. most web services ask for English users

    D. English is the most important language in the world

3. In the business world, who does not use English when doing business? _____

    A. Almost no one.   B. Non-English speakers.

    C. Mexican engineers.   D. Chinese experts.

4. Among the more than two hundred countries in the world, English is spoken in about _____.

   A. one-fifth of the countries
   B. one-fourth of the countries
   C. one-third of the countries
   D. half of the countries

5. Which of the following advantages of learning English the author suggests except? _____

   A. Access to Knowledge and Information.
   B. Advancing Your Career.
   C. Entertainment.
   D. Stress Reduction.

Module Ⅲ   Building up More Skills

Section A   Grammar Tips

Verb Tense(动词时态)

英语中,不同时间发生的动作或存在的状态,要用不同的**动词形式**来表示。这种不同的动词形式称作**时态**。

动作发生或状态存在的时间有**现在、过去、将来和过去将来**4 种,而发生或存在的方式也有**一般、进行、完成和完成进行**4 种。这样组合起来,英语就有 16 种时态,其动词基本形式列表如下。

	一般	进行	完成	完成进行
现在	do does	am/is/are doing	have/has done	have/has been doing
过去	did	was/were doing	had done	had been doing
将来	shall/will do	shall/will be doing	shall/will have done	shall/will have been doing
过去将来	should/would do	should/would be doing	should/would have done	should/would have been doing

Unit 1　Freshman

1. 现在进行时（The Present Continuous Tense）

表示说话时正在进行的动作,也可表示现阶段正在进行的动作。现在进行时由助动词 be 的现在时形式（am/is/are）加现在分词构成。

如：I'm looking for my umbrella right now. 我此刻正在找我的雨伞。

He is studying Chinese in Beijing. 他目前在北京学习中文。

2. 过去进行时（The Past Progressive Tense）

表示过去某一时刻正在进行的动作,或过去某一段时间内正在进行的动作。过去进行时是由助动词 be 的过去时形式（was/were）加现在分词构成。

如：I was sleeping at 2:00 yesterday afternoon. 昨天下午两点钟的时候我正在睡觉。

They were playing basketball while I was doing my homework. 他们在打篮球而我在做作业。

3. 现在完成时（The Present Perfect Tense）

表示过去的动作持续到现在并且已经完成,对现在造成的影响（并且动作可能持续发生下去）,由助动词 have/has 加动词过去分词构成。

如：The taxi has arrived. 出租车已经到了。

Our family has owned that house for generations. 我们家拥有这房子已经历经好几代人了。

常用：for + 一段时间（已经多久了）, since + 时间点（自从什么时候）

如：I have been there for 6 months. 我在那里已经6个月了。

I have lived here since 2010. 我从2010年就一直住在这里。

Miss Li has been in hospital since last week. 李小姐从上星期就住院了。

4. 过去完成时（The Past Perfect Tense）

表示过去某时前已发生的动作或情况（也可说是"过去的过去"）。由 had 加动词过去分词构成。

如：We had already learned two thousand words by the end of last year.

到去年年底我们已经学了2 000个单词。

5. 现在完成进行时（The Present Perfect Progressive Tense）

表示动作从过去某一时间开始,一直持续到现在,或者刚刚终止,或者可能仍然要继续下去。其构成为：主语+助动词（have/has）+been+动词的现在分词。

如：I have been working here for five years.

我已经在这里工作5年了。（动作还将继续下去）

I have been writing a book.

我一直在写一本书。（动作还将继续下去）

6. 过去将来时（The Past Future Tense）

表示过去将要发生的动作或情况,一般由助动词 should/would+动词原形构成,也可由 was/were going to+动词原形, was/were about to+动词原形构成。

如：I said on Thursday I should see my friend the next day.

我星期四说过我将于第二天拜访我的朋友。

When we were children, we would go swimming every summer.

我们小的时候,每年夏天都去游泳。

Practical Tasks

Task 1 Complete the following sentences.

1. She is very lazy and never _____ early at weekends.
   A. get up   B. getting up   C. gets up   D. got up
2. Don't talk here. Grandfather _____.
   A. is sleeping   B. are sleeping   C. sleep   D. sleeps
3. Bad weather _____ my summer holiday last year.
   A. spoil   B. spoils   C. spoiling   D. spoilt
4. —How did the accident happen?
   —You know, it _____ difficult to see the road clearly because it _____.
   A. was; was raining   B. is; has rained
   C. is; is raining   D. will be; will rain
5. Mr. Black _____ in China since five years ago.
   A. lived   B. has lived   C. lives   D. have lived
6. You _____ me waiting for two hours. I _____ for you since 5 o'clock.
   A. kept; waited   B. have kept; waited
   C. kept; have waited   D. had kept; have waited
7. He asked me where I _____ during the summer holidays.
   A. had been   B. had gone   C. went   D. was
8. He _____ to play the piano before he was 11 years old.
   A. learns   B. learned   C. has learned   D. had learned
9. —I have got a headache.
   —No wonder. You _____ in front of that computer too long.
   A. work   B. are working
   C. have been working   D. worked
10. Jerry told me he _____ on an old man's eyes in the hospital this Sunday.
    A. will operate   B. would operate
    C. operated   D. has operated

Task 2 Fill in each blank with the proper form of the given words.

1. He _____ (live) in Beijing now, but 5 years ago he _____ (live) in New York.
2. The river _____ (flow) very fast today—much faster than usual.
3. He first _____ (meet) his wife when they both _____ (be) in Beijing.
4. Hurry up! The train just _____ (come) in.
5. I _____ (make) dinner last night when the phone _____ (ring).
6. Our computer was broken and we hoped the new one _____ (arrive) soon.

7. During the winter I decided that I _____ (grow) tomatoes when the summer came.
8. The performance _____ (begin) when someone started crying.
9. They _____ (not come) to our party yesterday, even though we _____ (send) them a special invitation.
10. You know, I _____ (look) for a job for three months, and this is my first formal interview.

Section B Practical Writing

Letter(书信)

Writing Tips

英文书信分为私人信函和业务信函两类,一般都包括以下6个必要部分。

1. **信头(Heading or Letter-head)**

   指写信人的地址和写信日期,一般写在信纸的右上角。地址按从小到大的顺序书写。对于日期,英国人通常按照日、月、年的顺序写,而美国人通常按照月、日、年的顺序写。

2. **信内地址(Inside Address)**

   指收信人的姓名和地址,一般从日期下两行、信纸的左边写起。

3. **称呼语(Salutation)**

   指对收信人的称谓。顶格写起,自成一行。末尾用逗号或冒号。若知道对方姓名就用 Dear Mr./Mrs./Miss/Ms. 加上姓;若不知道对方姓名,则用 Dear Sir, Dear Madam;若对方职务较高,最好用其职务名称,如:Dear Prof. Smith。

4. **正文(Body of Letter)**

   指信函的主体部分,要求正文层次分明、简单易懂。通常为一事一段。开头应空4个字符左右。

5. **结束语(Complimentary Close)**

   结束语与称呼语相对应。结束语用"Yours faithfully,""Yours sincerely,"或"Yours,"等。

6. **署名(Signature)**

   位于结束语的下方。署名要求姓和名隔开,姓和名的首字母都需大写。

Sample

150 Heping St.
Shanghai, China
April 19, 2022

Maria
Australia

Dear Maria,

  Thank you for your letter and wonderful stamps. They are so nice. I like them very much.

  It is one year since I began to study in university. I take an active part in some activities and work hard on all courses. Whenever I meet with difficulties in study, I discuss them with my friends and try our best to solve them.

  The College English Test is coming. We are all busy preparing for it. I hope I can pass it.

  Please write back soon and give my best regards to your parents.

Yours,
Li Ming

Practical Tasks

Task 1 Correction

Peking University
2022 November 28

Li Hua
U. S. A.

Hello Mary,

  I missed you so much. Are you settled in yet? Have you met any of your new friends? I had to prepare for the English exam, I felt very tired these days. Fortunately, the exam is over, so I got time to write to you.

  Be sure to write back soon. I'm eager to hear from you. Take care of yourself.

Yours,
Li hua

Task 2　Writing

假设你是王伟,请写一封寄给你在美国的朋友布莱尔,向他介绍中国的春节,并邀请他来中国做客。

Module Ⅳ　Leisure Time

Dream
—Tagore(泰戈尔)

Dream is a beacon, guiding the direction of life.
A man without dreams is like a bird without wings;
A man without dreams is like a ship losing its direction.
Facing the sun, it will be hope;
Brave growth is a sharp edge.
I believe that dreams are the best faith.
It guides me forward and makes me stop wandering.
Even if the road ahead is full of thorns, there are many difficulties;
Even in the face of failure, pain and struggle.
As long as you make strong wings, you can fly against the wind;
As long as hope is turned into strength, miracles will fall from the sky.
I believe that I am who I am.
Unique and unstoppable;
Not afraid of loneliness, not afraid of wind and waves.
Because of you, side by side with me.

I believe in striding forward towards dreams.
We can change the world, we can realize our dreams.
I believe I can!

UNIT 2

Traditional Festival

Unit 2　Traditional Festival

Learning Objectives

Students should be able to
★　Understand the dialogues and passage by listening.
★　Talk about the Traditional Festivals in China.
★　Master the new words and expressions.
★　Review the Object Clauses.
★　Learn how to write an E-mail in English.

Module Ⅰ　Listening

Task 1　Listen to the following conversations twice and choose the best answer to each question you hear in the recording.

1. A. Yes, of course.　　　　　　　　　B. By train.
   C. See you again.　　　　　　　　　D. It doesn't matter.
2. A. Don't mention it.　　　　　　　　B. Let's go.
   C. Okay.　　　　　　　　　　　　　D. This way, please.
3. A. Prepare a speech.　　　　　　　　B. Book a ticket.
   C. Send an E-mail.　　　　　　　　　D. Make a phone call.
4. A. The Marketing Department.　　　　B. The Production Department.
   C. The Sales Department.　　　　　　D. The Engineering Department.
5. A. It is easy to repair.　　　　　　　　B. It often breaks down.
   C. It is very expensive.　　　　　　　D. It works fine.

Task 2　Listen to the following passage twice and fill in the blanks with the missing words you hear in the recording.

　　Ladies and gentlemen, our plane is flying smoothly now. The duty-free sales will soon begin. Please ___6___ your list of purchases. In your seat pocket, you can find the *Shopping on Board* magazine. All prices are listed both in the local currency(货币) and in US dollars. And you can pay ___7___ or by using a credit card. We accept ___8___ major credit cards. Frequent passengers win points ___9___ on board. There are some excellent bargains and there are several items specially designed for our ___10___. Thank you!

Module Ⅱ   Spotlight on Reading

Text A   Intensive Reading

Double Ninth Festival

1   When clear and **refreshing** autumn arrives, it's a time for the Chinese Chongyang Festival or Double Ninth Festival.

2   The Double Ninth Festival falls on the ninth day of the ninth month on the Chinese lunar calendar. In Chinese **folklore**, the number nine is the largest number, it's a **homonym** to the Chinese word jiu, which contains the **auspicious** meaning of "a long and healthy life".

3   In 1989, the Chinese government **designated** the Double Ninth Festival as the "Festival for the Elderly" to express wishes for health and **longevity** of the senior citizens. The Law on the Protection of the Rights and Interests of the Elderly, which has been in effect since 2013 clearly **stipulates** that every year's Double Ninth Festival is a legal festival for senior citizens.

4   In ancient times, it was **customary** to climb mountains to pray for good luck and longevity on the Double Ninth Festival. Every year at the Double Ninth Festival, people will climb up to the Tengwang **Pavilion** to enjoy the beautiful autumn **scenery** of the sea **melting** into the sky. Nowadays, the custom of climbing mountains for **blessings** on the Double Ninth Festival has gradually merged with some other outdoor exercises. Some activities have become especially popular among middle aged and older people such as Tai Chi, Qigong and Square Dancing.

5   Thanks to social care from their surroundings and love from there families, a growing number of seniors have begun to pay more attention to their later years. In recent years travel has become a very popular way for senior Chinese people to spend their leisure time. "The Sunset Glow Tour Group" referring to Chinese elders has gradually become a **trendy** word. Time has not stopped them from exploring the world and the elders who love life **deserve** the attention and respect of society. (296 words)

Unit 2　Traditional Festival

New Words

refreshing	/rɪˈfreʃɪŋ/	adj.	别有韵致的；给人新鲜感的
folklore	/ˈfəʊkˌlɔː(r)/	n.	民间传说
homonym	/ˈhɒmənɪm/	n.	同音异义词；同形异义词
auspicious	/ɔːˈspɪʃəs/	adj.	吉兆的；吉利的
designate	/ˈdezɪɡneɪt/	v.	选定；指派
longevity	/lɒnˈdʒevəti/	n.	长命；长寿
stipulate	/ˈstɪpjuleɪt/	v.	规定；约定
customary	/ˈkʌstəməri/	adj.	照习惯法的；照惯例的
pavilion	/pəˈvɪljən/	n.	阁楼
scenery	/ˈsiːnəri/	n.	风景；景色
melt	/melt/	v.	溶解；逐渐消失
blessing	/ˈblesɪŋ/	n.	上帝赐福；上帝保佑
trendy	/ˈtrendi/	adj.	时髦的；赶时髦的
deserve	/dɪˈzɜːv/	v.	应受；应得；值得

Phrases and Expressions

in effect 实际上
merge with 合并
thanks to 多亏了
pay attention to 注意,留心
refer to 提到,涉及

Inquiry Learning

1. **Double Ninth Festival** 重阳节,农历九月初九,二九相重,称为"重九",民间在该日有登高的风俗,所以重阳节又称"登高节"。还有重九节、茱萸节、菊花节等说法。由于九月初九"九九"谐音是"久久",有长久之意,所以常在此日祭祖与推行敬老活动。2012 年 12 月 28 日,修订 2013 年起施行的《中华人民共和国老年人权益保障法》(简称《老年人权益保障法》)明确每年农历九月初九为老年节。

2. **Lunar Calendar** 农历。农历是我国采用的一种传统历法,又名夏历、中历、旧历,民间也有称阴历的。它用严格的朔望周期定月,又用设置闰月的办法使年的平均长度与回归年相近,兼有阴历月和阳历年的性质,因此在实质上是一种阴阳合历。

3. **The Law on the Protection of the Rights and Interests of the Elderly, which has been in effect since 2013 clearly stipulates that every year's Double Ninth Festival is a legal festival for senior citizens.** 自 2013 年起施行的《老年人权益保障法》明确规定,每年的重阳节是老年人的法定节日。
   "which has been in effect"为非限制性定语从句,which 为关系代词,"the law on the Protection of the Rights and Interests of the Elderly"为先行词。
   "that every year's Double Ninth Festival is a legal festival for senior citizens"为宾语从句。

4. **The Sunset Glow Tour Group** 夕阳红旅游团。
   referring to Chinese elders 为动名词短语做后置定语,修饰"The Sunset Glow Tour Group"。

Reading Comprehension

Choose the best answer according to the passage.

1. What time is the Chinese Chongyang Festival? _____
   A. 9th September Lunar month.   B. 9th September Solar month.
   C. 9th October Lunar month.   D. 9th October Solar month.
2. What is the meaning of the Double Ninth Festival in Chinese folklore? _____
   A. A happy and long life.   B. A healthy and long life.

Unit 2 Traditional Festival

C. A wealthy and healthy life.   D. A happy and wealthy life.

3. When did the Chinese government assigned the Double Ninth Festival as the "Festival for the elderly"? _____
   A. In 1986.   B. In 1987.   C. In 1988.   D. In 1989.
4. What is customary to do in old time on the Double Ninth Festival? _____
   A. Play Tai Chi, Qigong and Square Dancing to keep a healthy and long life.
   B. Travel around the country to keep a happy and healthy life.
   C. Run Marathon to keep a healthy and strong life.
   D. Climb mountains to pray for good luck and longevity.
5. The best attitude towards the Double Ninth Festival concluded from this passage is _____.
   A. a negative attitude   B. a positive attitude
   C. an arrogant attitude   D. a selfish attitude

Language in Use

Task 1 Find the right definition in column B that matches the words in column A.

Column A	Column B
1. auspicious	A. very fashionable
2. longevity	B. show signs that sth. is likely to be successful
3. trendy	C. the traditions and stories of a country or community
4. scenery	D. long life; the fact of lasting a long time
5. designate	E. the natural features of an area, such as mountains, valleys, rivers and forests
6. folklore	F. to say officially that sth. has a particular character; to describe sth. in a particular way

Task 2 Fill in the blanks with the given words or expressions. Change the form where necessary.

deserve	in effect	refreshing	merge with	customary	pavilion

1. _____ drinks are in high demand as the temperature is 35 degrees Celsius.
2. When in New York City, it is _____ for the visitor to take in a Broadway show.
3. You don't _____ to have such true and loyal friends.
4. The two small banks _____ a larger one last year.
5. _____, favorable policies are to encourage employees' professional development.
6. Photo shows the night view of the China _____.

Translation

Task 1 Translate the following sentences from Chinese into English with the phrases given in the brackets.

1. 多亏了你的帮助,我在数学上不断取得进步。(thanks to)

2. 得到友谊的关键是关注别人的优点。(pay attention to)

3. 这位老兵提到了他在长征中的经历。(refer to)

4. 合同上规定工人们应领计件工资。(stipulate)

5. 他的剧作家生涯有一个好的开头。(auspicious)

Task 2 Translate the following sentences from English into Chinese.

1. Fiber from fruit had no impact on longevity.

2. Fishermen's folklore says men and women cannot die while the tide is rising.

3. The region is remarkable for its woodland scenery.

4. With the temperature rising, polar ice will melt at a faster rate.

5. Is it customary to tip hairdressers in this country?

Text B Extensive Reading

Double Seventh Festival

1 The seventh day of the seventh Lunar month is Qixi, widely regarded as China's Valentine's Day. Many different stories lay claim to being the origin of the festival but one **version** is the most popular and accepted.

2 The youngest daughter of the Jade Emperor(the ruler of the world in legend), the Weaver Girl was a **fairy** who **weaved** rosy clouds in the sky. She became tired of the boring **immortal** life and decided to descend to the mortal world. she met and fell in love with a cowherd. The Jade Emperor strongly objected to the couple's union and forcibly separated them by the Milky Way leaving them torn apart by the **galaxy** and only allowing them to meet once a year.

Unit 2　Traditional Festival

3　Despite that, the distance could not stop their love for one another. They still love each other and look forward to meeting once a year on the seventh day of the seventh lunar month.

4　On Qixi, more and more young people are going on dates and exchanging gifts to express their **affection**. This in turn gave rise to a unique Qixi **economy**. Long queues are also often formed at the gate of the Civil Affairs Bureau where couples rush to **register** for marriage when love is in air. This is because Qixi carries with it a **symbolic** meaning, choose your own love and remain **faithful** for life.

5　More than 2,000 years ago, Qixi also known as "the Begging Festival". In ancient China, women would visit their close friends and **worship** the Weaver Girl on the seventh day of the seventh lunar month praying they could become as clever as the Weaver Girl and find their faithful lover. In traditional Chinese marriage, women who pray for **dexterity** often devote all their energies to family life.

6　However, times have changed as the role of women has transformed. A more **diversified** social role enables women in China to **pursue** their love **courageously** and no longer be bound to **domestic** life like the Weaver Girl. (327 words)

New Words

version	/ˈvɜːrʒn/	n. 版本；译文
fairy	/ˈfeəri/	n. 仙女；小精灵
weave	/wiːv/	vt. 编织；纺织
immortal	/ɪˈmɔːtl/	adj. 不朽的；流芳百世的
descend	/dɪˈsend/	vi. 下降；下落
forcibly	/ˈfɔːsəbli/	adv. 强行地；强烈地
galaxy	/ˈɡæləksi/	n. 银河；星系
affection	/əˈfekʃn/	n. 喜爱；喜欢
economy	/ɪˈkɒnəmi/	n. 经济；节约
register	/ˈredʒɪstə/	v. 登记；注册
symbolic	/sɪmˈbɒlɪk/	adj. 象征的；符号的

faithful	/ˈfeɪθfəl/	adj. 忠诚的;忠实的;可靠的
worship	/ˈwɜːʃɪp/	vt. 崇拜;爱慕
dexterity	/dekˈsterəti/	n. 灵巧;机敏
diversified	/daɪˈvɜːsɪfaɪd/	adj. 多样化的;多种多样的
pursue	/pəˈsjuː/	vt. 追赶;追求
courageously	/kəˈreɪdʒəsli/	adv. 勇敢地
domestic	/dəˈmestɪk/	adj. 家庭的;国内的

Phrases and Expressions

tear apart 分开,裂开
look forward to 期盼,期待
devote to 忠于,致力于
be bound to 肯定,注定

Inquiry Learning

1. **The Jade Emperor strongly objected to the couple's union and forcibly separated them by the Milky Way leaving them torn apart by the galaxy and only allowing them to meet once a year.** 玉皇大帝强烈反对这对夫妇的结合,并强行用银河系将他们分开,只允许他们一年见一次面。
   "leaving them torn apart by the galaxy"和"only allowing them to meet once a year"为现在分词短语做伴随状语。
   torn apart 过去分词表被动,意为被分开。
   如:The dictionary was torn apart entirely. 这本字典被完全撕开了。
   　　Without being tidily torn apart. 出淤泥而不染。

2. **They still love each other and look forward to meeting once a year on the seventh day of the seventh lunar month.** 他们仍然彼此相爱,并期待着每年农历七月初七见一次面。
   Look forward to doing sth. 期待做某事,to 是介词。
   如:I look forward to meeting you at the airport. 我期望能在机场见到你。
   　　I look forward to hearing from you. 我期待收到你的来信。

3. **Women who pray for dexterity often devote all their energies to family life.** 祈求灵巧的女性往往把她们所有的精力都投入到家庭生活中。
   "who pray for dexterity"定语从句,先行词为 women。
   devote... to... 把……致力于……, to 为介词。
   如:He devotes his spare time to studying English translation.

他把业余时间都致力于学习英语翻译。

Reading Comprehension

Choose the best answer according to the passage.

1. What time is China's Valentine's Day? _____
   A. 7th July Lunar month.　　　　　B. 7th July Solar month.
   C. 14th February Lunar month.　　　D. 14th February Solar month.

2. Why did Weaver Girl go down to the mortal world? _____
   A. Because she fell in love with a boy in the mortal world.
   B. Because it was very interesting in the mortal world.
   C. Because she was tired of the boring life in the immortal world.
   D. Because the Jade Emperor forced her to the mortal world.

3. How will more and more young people do on Qixi? _____
   A. They will rush to the Civil Affairs Bureau to register for marriage.
   B. They will choose to travel with their lovers.
   C. They will celebrate the festival with their friends.
   D. They will celebrate the festival with each other.

4. What did Qixi call in ancient time? _____
   A. The Valentine's Day.　　　　　B. The Begging Festival.
   C. The Lover's Day.　　　　　　　D. The Couple's Day.

5. What's the main idea of the passage? _____
   A. Introduce a traditional festival Qixi.
   B. Introduce a Weaver Girl and Cowherd's loving story.
   C. Introduce how Weaver Girl and Cowherd meet each other.
   D. Introduce the customs of Qixi.

Module Ⅲ　Building up More Skills

Section A　Grammar Tips

Objective Clauses（宾语从句）

宾语从句:在句子中起宾语作用的从句叫宾语从句。宾语从句分为3类:动词的宾语从句、介词的宾语从句和形容词的宾语从句。根据作用的不同,宾语从句的引导词通常分为以下几类。

连接词	词义	功能
that	无词义	不做成分,只起连接作用,口语中可省略
whether/if	是否	不做成分,但不能省略
what, which, who, whose 等连接代词	什么、哪个、谁、谁的	做主语、宾语、表语、定语等
when, where, why, how 等连接副词	表时间、地点、原因、方式等	做状语

知识点1:宾语从句的连接词的用法

常用的连接词有:that, if, whether, what, which, who, whom, when, where, how, why 等。

1.【要点】宾语从句是陈述句时,用 that 引导。在口语中 that 常被省略。

如:I know(that) you are a student.

2.【要点】宾语从句是一般疑问句时,用 if 或 whether 来引导。If, whether 意为"是否",whether 还可以与 or not 连用。

如:Lily wanted to know if her grandma liked the handbag.

莉莉想知道她的祖母是否喜欢这个手提袋。

3.【要点】宾语从句是特殊疑问句时,用疑问词引导。

如:He didn't tell me where he was going.

他没告诉我他想去哪儿。

Can you tell me what he said just now? 你能告诉我他刚才说了什么吗?

知识点2:宾语从句的语序

1.【要点】陈述句变为宾语从句时,要注意人称和时态的变化,语序不变。

如:She said, "I will leave a message on the desk."

她说她会在桌上留口信的。

She said that she would leave a message on the desk.

2.【要点】一般疑问句和特殊疑问句变为宾语从句时,也要注意人称和时态的变化,后面接陈述句语序。

如:"Where are the tickets?" I asked him.

我问他票在哪儿。

I asked him where the tickets were.

注意:宾语从句的人称要遵循"一随主、二随宾、第三人称不更新"的原则。如下表:

直接引语的主语	变为间接引语后
第一人称	与主句的主语一致
第二人称	与主句的宾语一致
第三人称	不变

知识点 3：宾语从句的时态

1.【要点】如果主句是一般现在时、一般将来时或祈使句，宾语从句的时态不受限制，可以根据实际表达的需要来确定。

　　如：Could you tell me what he said at the meeting?

　　　　你能告诉我他在会上说了什么吗？

　　　　He will tell us that he has been able to look after himself.

　　　　他会告诉我们他已经能照顾自己。

　　　　Tell him when we will finish our work.

　　　　告诉他我们将什么时候完成工作。

2.【要点】如果主句是过去的某种时态，宾语从句应与主句保持一致，用过去的某种时态。

　　如：He said that he was born in Wenzhou in 1996.

　　　　他说他 1996 年出生于温州。

　　　　They said that they had already seen the film.

　　　　他们说他们已经看过这部电影了。

3.【要点】如果宾语从句所叙述的是客观事实、格言、科学真理时，从句时态不受主句限制，用一般现在时。

　　如：Everyone knew there are 365 days in a year.

　　　　大家都知道一年有 365 天。

　　　　She said that two heads are better than one.

　　　　她说三个臭皮匠顶个诸葛亮。

知识点 4：宾语从句的否定前移

【要点】在宾语从句中，当主句的谓语动词为 think, believe, expect, imagine, suppose 等，主语为 I 或 we 时，从句中表示否定意义的 not 应移到 think, believe, expect, imagine, suppose 等前。

　　如：I don't suppose he will come.

　　　　我猜他不会来。

注意：如果主句主语不是 I 或 we，则 not 不前移。

　　如：She thinks she can't arrive there on time.

　　　　她认为她不能按时到那儿。

知识点 5：宾语从句的简化

1.【要点】当宾语从句的主语和主句的主语相同，且谓语动词是 hope, wish, decide 等时，从句可简化为不定式结构。

如：I hope that I can see you again.

＝I hope to see you again. 我希望能再次见到你.

2.【要点】当宾语从句的主语和主句的主语相同,且谓语动词是 know,remember, forget,learn 等时,从句可简化为"疑问词+不定式"结构。

如：I don't know what I should say.

＝I don't know what to say. 我不知道该说什么。

3.【考查点】当主句的谓语动词是 ask,tell,show,teach 等,且宾语从句的主语和主句的间接宾语一致时,从句可简化为不定式结构或"疑问词+不定式"结构。

如：Mr. Hu tells us that we shouldn't draw on the wall.

＝Mr. Hu tells us not to draw on the wall. 胡老师告诉我们不应该在墙上画画。

Practical Tasks

Task 1　Complete the following sentences with object clauses.

1. —Can you tell me _____ to London?
   —Sure. Next month.
   A. when you will travel　　　　B. when will you travel
   C. when you travelled　　　　　D. when did you travel

2. —Could you tell me _____?
   —At nine o'clock, in ten minutes.
   A. how will he leave　　　　　B. when he has left
   C. why he is leaving　　　　　D. when he will leave

3. —Can you tell me _____?
   —He lives in Shanghai.
   A. where Mark lives　　　　　B. where does Mark live
   C. where Mark lived　　　　　D. where did Mark live

4. —Could you tell me _____ his hometown?
   —The day after tomorrow, I think.
   A. when will you visit　　　　B. when you will visit.
   C. why you will visit　　　　　D. how you will visit.

5. —Do you know _____?
   —Let me see. I remember it was on March 18th.
   A. why did they move here　　B. why they moved here
   C. when did they move here　 D. when they moved here

6. —Excuse me. Could you tell me _____ about the local history and culture?
   —Of course. You can check it on this computer.
   A. how can I get the information　　B. what information did I get
   C. where I can get the information　D. that I got the information

7. —Daniel, could you tell me _____?
   —Certainly, in Brazil.
   A. when the 2016 Olympics will be held　　B. when will the 2016 Olympics be held
   C. where the 2016 Olympics will be held　　D. where will the 2016 Olympics be held

8. I don't know if you _____ to Mary's party next Sunday. If you go, _____.
   A. go; so will I   B. will go; so will I
   C. will go; so do I   D. go; so do I
9. —Would you like to tell me _____?
   —Sure. Practice makes perfect.
   A. how can I learn English better   B. how I can learn English better
   C. why can I learn English better   D. why I can learn English better
10. —I am worried about _____.
    —Whatever the result is, don't be too hard on yourself.
    A. how have I prepared for my final exams
    B. if I can get great grads in the final exams
    C. that my school team lost the game because of my fault
    D. why did my school team lose the game
11. There are so many foggy days recently. We all wonder _____.
    A. how is the air polluted   B. why the air is seriously polluted
    C. what can we do to prevent that bad weather   D. what are the real reasons
12. —What did Max just say to you?
    —He asked me _____.
    A. if I would like to go skating   B. when did I buy this CD
    C. where I will spend the weekend   D. that I had a good time
13. —Do you know _____ this afternoon?
    —I'm not sure, but I'll tell you as soon as she comes.
    A. how will Betty arrive   B. what time Betty will arrive
    C. where Betty will arrive   D. whether will Betty arrive

Task 2 Fill in an appropriate conjunctive pronoun or adverb for each blanks.
1. Could you tell me _____ the nearest hospital is?
2. I want to know _____ she is looking after.
3. The small children don't know _____ is in their stockings.
4. I don't know _____ he will come tomorrow.
5. I can't understand _____ Christmas means.

Section B Practical Writing

E-mail（电子邮件）

Writing Tips

英文电子邮件的基本要素是主题、称谓、正文、结尾用语及署名。

首先，标题(Heading)栏的"收件人"(To)框中必须输入收信人的E-mail地址。电子邮件中最重要的部分是"主题"，在打开邮箱阅读邮件时，第一眼看到的就是邮件的"主题",所以"主题"(Subject)框的内容应简明地概括信的内容,短的可以是一个单词,如greetings;长的可以是一个名词性短语,也可以是一个完整句,但长度一般不超过35个字母。"主题"框的内容切忌含糊不清。像"News about the meeting"这样的表达,应改为"Tomorrow's meeting canceled"。一般来说,只要将位于句首的单词和专有名词的首字母大写即可。另外一种较为正规的格式可将除了少于5个字母的介词、连接词或冠词之外的每一个单词的首字母大写,如"New E-mail Address Notification"。视信的内容是否重要,还可以在开头加上 URGENT 或者 FYI(For Your Information,供参考),如"URGENT: Submit your report today!"。

　　E-mail 一般使用非正式的文体,因此正文(Body)前的称呼(Salutation)通常无须使用诸如"Dear Mr. John"之类的表达。对同辈的亲朋好友或同事可以直呼其名,但对长辈或上级最好使用头衔加上姓。如:Tommy 或者 Mr. Smith. 。

　　E-mail 文体的另外一个特点是简单明了,便于阅读,太长的内容可以以附件的方式发出。一个段落大多仅由一到三个句子组成。信尾客套话(Complimentary Close)通常也很简明,常常只需一个词,如:"Thanks""Best""Cheers"。不需要用一般信函中的"Sincerely yours"或"Best regards"。称呼和正文之间、段落之间、正文和信尾客套话之间一般空一行,开头无须空格。如:

Jimmy,
I received your memo and will discuss it with Eric on Wednesday.
Best,
David

　　E-mail 的非正式的文体特点并不意味着它的撰写可以马虎,给长辈或者上级写信,或者撰写业务信函更是如此。写完信后,一定要认真检查有无拼写、语法和标点符号错误。

Sample 1

From: Liugang@qq.com
To: JohnsonSmith@qq.com
Date: 3-July-2018
Subject: Application for the position of the Sales Manager
Attached: Resume
Dear Mr. Smith,

　　Thanks for your mail informing me of the position of Sales Manager in China, I am interested in this position and want to have further detailed discussion about it. Enclosed please find my resume in Chinese and English. I look forward to an interview in Wuhan ASAP.

　　Best wishes.

Sincerely yours,
Liu Gang

Unit 2 Traditional Festival

Sample 2

From：Zhangli@ hotmail. com

To：Joanna@ hotmail. com

Date：1-June-2018

Subject：the opening of a sample room

Dear Joanna,

　　Mr. John Green, our General Manager, will be in Paris from June 2 to 7 and would like to come and see you on June 3 about the opening of a sample room there. Please let us know if the time is convenient for you. If not, what time you would suggest.

Yours faithfully,
Zhang Li

Practical Tasks

Task You are required to write an E-mail according to the following instructions given in Chinese.

发信人邮件地址：Liujun11067@ 163. com

收件人邮件地址：Anna110068@ 163. com

日期：2022 年 10 月 28 日

主题：www. ebay. com. cn 所售的书(书名：《走遍中国》，买家是美国客户安娜·布朗)

谢谢您订购《走遍中国》。您所订购的书已经发出，您将在约一周的时间内收到。希望您收到书后能在我们网站上对我们的服务做出评价，如果您觉得满意请向您的朋友推荐我们。我们将有更多的新书上市，如果您再次光临购书，我们将给予您折扣。

Module Ⅳ   Leisure Time

English Film
Kung Fu Panda

(Master Shifu learns the bad news, and he returns to Oogway for help, but Oogway passes away, and tells him to believe in Po.)

Master: The panda? Master, that panda is not the Dragon Warrior. He wasn't even meant to be here! It was an accident.

Oogway: There are no accidents.

Master: Yes, I know. You've said that already. Twice.

Oogway: Well. That was no accident, either.

Master: Thrice.

Oogway: My old friend, the panda will never fulfill his destiny nor yours, until you let go of the illusion of control.

Master: Illusion?

Oogway: Yes. Look at this tree, Shifu. I cannot make it blossom when it suits me nor make it bear fruit before its time.

Master: But there are things we can control. I can control when the fruit will fall. And I can control where to plant the seed. That is no illusion, Master.

Oogway: Yes. But no matter what you do that seed will grow to be a peach tree. You may wish an apple or an orange but you will get a peach.

Master: But a peach cannot defeat Tai Lung!

Oogway: Maybe it can. If you are willing to guide it. To nurture it. To believe in it.

Master: But how? How? I need your help, Master.

Oogway: No, you just need to believe. Promise me, Shifu. Promise me you will believe.

Master: I will try.

Oogway: Good. My time has come. You must continue your journey without me.

Master: What are you? Wait! Master!

Unit 2　Traditional Festival

UNIT 3

Internet

Unit 3 Internet

Learning Objectives

Students should be able to
★ Understand the dialogues and passage by listening.
★ Talk about the Internet.
★ Master the new words and expressions.
★ Review the Non-finite Verb.
★ Learn how to write the Application for Scholarships and Assistantship in English.

Module Ⅰ Listening

Task 1 Listen to the following conversations twice and choose the best answer to each question you hear in the recording.

1. A. He's got a headache.   B. He coughs a lot.
   C. He can't sleep at night.   D. He doesn't feel like eating.
2. A. Have some food.   B. Make a phone call.
   C. Clean the table.   D. Buy a dictionary.
3. A. The sales manager.   B. The office secretary.
   C. The information officer.   D. The chief engineer.
4. A. Teacher and student.   B. Police officer and driver.
   C. Manager and secretary.   D. Husband and wife.
5. A. Asking the way.   B. Checking in at the airport.
   C. Buying a ticket.   D. Booking a room.

Task 2 Listen to the following passage twice and fill in the blanks with the missing words you hear in the recording.

Some managers have noticed recently that the employees in the company are __6__ the policy of having breaks. The workers have two 15-minute breaks per day. However, the two breaks are lasting __7__ 25 to 30 minutes each. The workers complain that the factory work is so __8__ that they need longer breaks. Also the dining hall is so far away that it takes too long to walk there and back. But the company is losing hundreds of work hours each year. Should employees __9__ the time they are not working? The general manager has to call a meeting to __10__ this matter.

Module Ⅱ Spotlight on Reading

Text A Intensive Reading

The Popular Internet

1   In modern society, computers are being used by more and more people, and the Internet has been widely used in various fields, including **military**, film, medicine, media and so on. With the **application** of computer and the Internet, information has entered a stage of rapid development. Moreover, the Internet technology is getting better and faster. What's more, the most exciting thing is the economic **boom** brought by the Internet.

2   A new **poll** shows that people believe that computers and the Internet have made life better for people. The man who was interviewed said that he wouldn't stand if computers and the Internet disappeared in his world. But they also see some dangers in the trend toward **computerization**.

3   The poll found that the public **favors** some government protection from **cyber** problems but in general people are not especially concerned about **issues** such as information **overload** or the never-ending flow of phone calls, **faxes** and E-mails. A **separate** survey of children aged 10 ~ 17 shows that they have a more positive attitude about computers than adults do, and most have made use of up-to-date technology in their schools, they use computers to finish their homework assigned by their teachers, they can also use the Internet to listen the famous professors' lessons. Some students think it is convenient for them to buy some daily necessities and school supplies.

4   The survey found that **enthusiasm** for computers and the Internet is found in all income groups, all **regions** of the country, all **races**, and most age groups. However, people over 60 and those towards the lower end of the income rank tend to show lower rates of computer **ownership** and Internet **usage**. The survey shows that "some kind of **gap** has been crossed: Computers are part of everyday life for most people, and the Internet is close behind." (305 words)

Unit 3　Internet

New Words

military	/ˈmɪlɪtəri/	n.	军事；军方
application	/ˌæplɪˈkeɪʃn/	n.	申请
boom	/buːm/	n.	繁荣
poll	/pəʊl/	n.	民意调查；选举投票
trend	/trend/	n.	趋势；热门话题
computerization	/kəmˌpjutəraɪˈzeɪʃn/	n.	电脑化
favor	/ˈfeɪvə/	v.	比较喜欢；有利于；帮助
cyber	/ˈsaɪbə/	adj.	与计算机有关的
issue	/ˈɪʃuː/	n.	议题；争论点；发表
overload	/ˌəʊvəˈləʊd/	v.	超载；负担过重
fax	/fæks/	n.	传真机
separate	/ˈsepərət/	adj.	单独的
enthusiasm	/ɪnˈθjuːziæzəm/	n.	热情
income	/ˈɪnkʌm/	n.	收入；收益
region	/ˈriːdʒən/	n.	地区；区域

43

race	/reɪs/	n.	赛跑;人种;竞赛
ownership	/ˈəʊnəʃɪp/	n.	所有权
usage	/ˈjuːsɪdʒ/	n.	用法
gap	/gæp/	n.	缝隙;缺口

Phrases and Expressions

in general 总之,通常
make use of 充分利用
concern about... 对……担心
flow of... ……的流动

Inquiry Learning

1. **The poll found that the public favors some government protection from cyber problems, but in general people are not especially concerned about issues such as information overload or the never-ending flow of phone calls, faxes and e-mails.**
   这次民意调查发现公众非常希望政府能够保护他们免受网络问题的侵扰,但是人们通常不大关心诸如信息超载、没完没了的电话、传真和电子邮件等问题。
   that 引导的是宾语从句,"the public favors some government protection from cyber problems"做 found 的宾语。

2. **A separate survey of children aged 10~17 shows that they have a more positive attitude about computers than adults do, and most have made use of up-to-date technology in their schools.**
   一项对年龄在10~17岁之间的儿童单独进行的调查显示,他们对电脑的态度比成年人积极,而且他们大多数曾经都用过先进的技术。
   aged 10~17 过去分词短语做后置定语,修饰前面的名词 children。
   "that they have a more positive attitude about computers than adults do"是由关系代词 that 引导的宾语从句,做 shows 的宾语。

3. **However, people over 60 and those towards the lower end of the income rank tend to show lower rates of computer ownership and Internet usage.**
   然而,60岁以上的老人和那些收入较低的人群表明了较低的电脑持有率和互联网使用率。
   这是一个较难理解的复杂句,"people over 60 and those towards the lower end of the income rank"做主语,"tend to show"做谓语,"lower rates of computer ownership and Internet usage"做宾语。

Unit 3 Internet

Reading Comprehension

Choose the best answer according to the passage.

1. The first paragraph shows that _____ .
   A. the new poll about computers and the Internet is helpful
   B. people should explore the dangers of computerization
   C. people can not do without computers and the Internet
   D. computerization has its advantages
2. The word "enthusiasm" is closet in meaning to _____ .
   A. great love   B. great hatred   C. problem   D. advantage
3. What are they concerned about according to the poll? _____
   A. Age of the children using the Internet.
   B. Government protection from the Internet problems.
   C. Information overload.
   D. The flow of phone calls, faxes and e-mails.
4. The teenagers tend to _____ than adults.
   A. care more about information overload   B. like using computers more
   C. dislike using computers more   D. face less danger
5. We can learn from the passage that _____ .
   A. all children have used the latest technology in schools
   B. computers and the Internet are very popular
   C. people tend to place more importance in the Internet usage than computers
   D. the public do not hate the Internet problems

Language in Use

Task 1 Find the right definition in column B that matches the words in column A.

Column A	Column B
1. usage	A. the steady and continuous movement of something or somebody in one direction
2. ownership	B. a space between two thing or in the middle of something
3. race	C. the action of using something or the fact of being used
4. concern	D. something that interests you because it is important or affect you
5. gap	E. the relationship of an owner to the thing possessed
6. flow	F. a situation in which groups compete to be first to achieve a goal

Task 2 Fill in the blanks with the given words or expressions. Change the form where necessary.

| poll | trend | favor | issue | income | gap |

1. Most people, in fact, _____ the lessening of prejudice.
2. The _____ remains hotly disputed.
3. The final result of the _____ will be known tomorrow.
4. This is a growing _____.
5. His death left an enormous _____ in my life.
6. He has a private _____.

Translation

Task 1 Translate the following sentences from Chinese into English with the phrases given in the brackets.

1. 该地区处于极其严重的经济衰退中。(region)

2. 你需要一个最新的网络浏览器。(up-to-date)

3. 我们都对他的热情留下深刻的印象。(enthusiasm)

4. 不要让船超载了,否则它会沉下去。(overload)

5. 这件事在三个不同的场合发生过。(separate)

Task 2 Translate the following sentences from English into Chinese.

1. The product has filled a gap in the market.

2. While listening, you can nod your head to show you in favor of his or her views.

3. Is there a cyber bar nearby?

4. Ownership of the land is currently being disputed.

5. She has watched the race on video.

Unit 3 Internet

Text B Intensive Reading

Beware of Online Scammers

1 With the development of the Internet, more and more people like to browse the web. They always shop online with mobile phones and computers. Furthermore, they use their mobile phones to pay for what they bought.

2 However, what should you do if you **discover** you are being **scammed**? The first thing is to stop all **contact** with the scammer. It is important to be **suspicious** because scammers have ways of making their **offers** seem real.

3 Beware of the false sense of **reassurance** that can come from **tricks** like these:

4 Scammers can **convincingly imitate** the logos and communication style of trusted companies. They are known to make **fake** websites to fool people into giving money or information.

5 Scams can come from within New Zealand. International scammers also use **fake location** data to **appear** as if they were in your city or country. An opportunity isn't necessarily safe just because someone uses a local telephone number or contact address.

6 Scammers can learn **private details** through computer **hacking** or by taking E-mail from your E-mail address. They use this information to build your trust. You have to be cautious about the information and try to identify the information if it has been leaked. If someone offering the opportunity knows a lot about you, it doesn't mean the opportunity is real.

7 Scammers *plays on people's emotions* and are experienced at building trust to **eventually exploit** the **relationship**. When you develop a relationship with someone over time, it can be harmful to think their interest in you may not be **sincere**. But if someone you met online eventually asks you to **send** or **receive** money, stop and think.

8 If you have noticed or been caught in a scam, report it to Netsafe. However, what should you do if you discover you have already been scammed? It would be **ignorant** if you contact with the scammer again. Don't try to recover your financial losses by yourself. What you should do is to make a list of losses, calling the police as soon as possible. (342 words)

New Words

discover	/dɪˈskʌvə/	v. 发现
scam	/skæm/	v. 诈骗
contact	/ˈkɒntækt/	v. 联系；接触
suspicious	/səˈspɪʃəs/	adj. 可疑的
offer	/ˈɒfə/	v. 提供；报价
reassurance	/ˌriːəˈʃʊərəns/	v. 保证；安慰
trick	/trɪk/	n. 花招；恶作剧；技巧
convincingly	/kənˈvɪnsɪŋli/	adv. 令人信服地
imitate	/ˈɪmɪteɪt/	v. 模仿；伪造
fake	/feɪk/	adj. 伪造的；假货

location	/ləʊˈkeɪʃən/	n.	地点；位置
appear	/əˈpɪə/	v.	出现；呈现
private	/ˈpraɪvət/	adj.	私人的；秘密的
detail	/ˈdiːteɪl/	n.	细节；详情
hack	/hæk/	v.	非法侵入
eventually	/ɪˈventʃuəli/	adv.	最终
exploit	/ɪkˈsplɔɪt/	v.	利用；开发
relationship	/rɪˈleɪʃ(ə)nʃɪp/	n.	关系；关联
sincere	/sɪnˈsɪə/	adj.	真诚的
online	/ˈɒnlaɪn/	adj.	网上的；联机的
send	/send/	v.	发送；派遣
receive	/rɪˈsiːv/	v.	收到；接待
ignorant	/ˈɪgnərənt/	adj.	无知的

Phrases and Expressions

browse the web 浏览网页
beware of... 对……谨慎
build one's trust 建立信任
over time 久而久之

Inquiry Learning

1. **It is important to be suspicious because scammers have ways of making their offers seem real.**
   由于诈骗者有方法让他们发出的通知看起来像真的一样，所以保持怀疑是很重要的。
   这个句子中 it 是形式主语，真正的主语是 to be suspicious，because 引导原因状语从句。

2. **... scammers also use fake location data to appear as if they were in your city or country.**
   诈骗者也会使用假定位数据出现，就好像他们在你所在的城市或者国家。
   由 as if 引导的从句用了虚拟语气，从句表示与现在事实相反，谓语动词一般用过去式，所以用 were。
   如：It isn't as if you were going away for good.
   　　又不是你离开不回来了。
   　　I can remember our wedding as if it were yesterday.
   　　我仍对我们的婚礼记忆犹新，就像发生在昨天一样。

3. **Scammers can learn private details through computer hacking or by taking email from your email address.**
   诈骗者可以通过计算机非法侵入或从电子邮箱地址获取邮件来得知你的私人资料。
   这个句子是一个简单句，scammers 是主语，learn 是谓语动词，private details 是宾语，through computer hacking or taking email from your email address 是方式状语。
   如：You will achieve your dream as long as you work hard.
   只要你努力，你就一定能够实现梦想的。
   The robber forced the old man to enter the room with a knife in his hand.
   这个强盗手里拿把小刀，强迫老人进入房间。
4. **When you develop a relationship with someone over time, it can be harmful to think their interest in you may not be sincere.**
   当你和某人发展了一段长时间的关系的时候，你认为他们对你的兴趣可能不是很真诚，这件事情会让你感觉很受伤害的。
   整个句子是一个复合性从句，"when you develop a relationship with someone overtime" 是由 when 引导的时间状语从句，"it can be harmful to think their interest in you may not be sincere" 这个句子中 it 是形式主语，真正的主语是后面的动词不定式，think 后面又接一个宾语从句，省略了关系代词 that。

Reading Comprehension

Choose the best answer according to the passage.

1. According to the passage, if you find you are being deceived, you should first _____.
   A. turn off your computer   B. look for an anti-virus app
   C. report it to the police officer D. stop contacting the scammer
2. To deceive people into giving money or information, scammers _____.
   A. make fake websites   B. pretend to be police officers
   C. imitate their signature   D. record their supervisor's voice
3. To make a call seem local, international scammers may _____.
   A. speak to you in your own language   B. ask their friends to make the call
   C. buy a cell phone from a local store D. use a fake local phone number
4. The expressions "play on people's emotions" in Paragraph 7 means _____.
   A. lack proper emotions   B. share others' emotions
   C. make unfair use of people's emotions D. pay no attention to people's emotions
5. What should you do if you discovered that you have been cheated? _____
   A. Report it to Netsafe.   B. Inform your parents.
   C. Contact with the scammer again. D. Make a list and call the police.

Unit 3　Internet

Module Ⅲ　Building up More Skills

Section A　Grammar Tips

Non-finite Verb(非谓语动词)

Non-finite Verb(非谓语动词)
一、非谓语动词的语法功能
　　英语非谓语动词指在句中不做谓语的动词。非谓语动词有3种：动词不定式、分词和动名词。非谓语动词有以下特点。
　　(1)在句中不能独立充当谓语，但具有动词的一般特征，即后面可跟宾语，可以被状语修饰，有时态、语态的变化。
　　(2)非谓语动词没有人称和数的变化。由于三者具有不同的语法功能，各自在句中充当的句子成分也不尽相同。其用法功能见下表。

	主语 Subject	宾语 Object	表语 Predicative	定语 Attribute	状语 Adverbial	宾语补语 Object Complement
不定式 (to do) Infinitive	☆	☆	☆	☆	☆	☆
分词(doing/done) Participial			☆	☆	☆	☆
动名词 (doing) Gerund	☆	☆	☆	☆		

Tips
　　1. 动名词具有名词性特征，在句中仅充当主语、宾语、表语和定语。分词主要具有形容词和副词的性质，在句中可充当表语、定语、状语和补语。不定式可用作主语、宾语、表语、定语、状语和补语。
　　2. 不定式和动名词都可以做主语、宾语、表语，其区别是不定式通常表示将来发生的、具体的、一次性的动作。动名词则表示经常性的、抽象的动作。
　　3. 不定式做定语时为短语形式需要后置，动名词做定语要放在被修饰词之前。

4. 现在分词往往表示动作是主动的或正在进行的,过去分词则表示被动的或已完成的概念。

5. 现在分词做定语表示被修饰的名词动作正在进行,动名词做定语表示所修饰名词的性质、用途或场所。

6. 现在分词做表语表示主语的特征或状态,动名词做表语可以同主语互换位置。

7. 现在分词做补语表示其逻辑主语的动作是主动、在进行,分词做补语表示其逻辑主语的动作是被动或完成。不定式做补语表示其逻辑主语的动作即将发生。

8. 分词做状语一般表示原因、时间、条件、伴随。不定式做状语表示目的、结果或原因。

二、非谓语动词的时态

非谓语动词有时态和语态的变化,见下表。

语态	主动语态			被动语态		
时态	不定式	分词	动名词	不定式	分词	动名词
一般时	to write	writing	writing	to be written	being written	being written
完成时	to have written	having written	having written	to have been written	having been written	having been written
进行时	to be writing					
完成进行时	to have been writing					

Tips

1. 不定式一般时表示的动作与谓语动词的动作同时发生或在谓语动词动作之后发生。

2. 不定式完成时表示的动作发生在谓语动词的动作之前。不定式进行时表示正在进行与谓语动词同时发生的动作。

3. 动名词与现在分词都只有一般时和完成时形式。一般时表示的动作与谓语动词的动作同时发生,完成时表示的动作皆发生在谓语动词动作之前。

4. 现在分词一般时被动与完成时被动同义,皆表示动作已完成。

5. 现在分词有其独立的逻辑主语,置于现在分词之前构成分词的独立主格结构,可位于句首或句末,常用作状语。

6. 过去分词一般表示完成或被动的动作,只有一种形式。

Practical Task

Task Choose the best answer to complete each of the following sentences.

1. _____ at in this way, the present economic situation doesn't seem so gloomy.
   A. Looking   B. Looked   C. Having looked   D. To look

2. There _____ nothing more for discussion, the meeting came to an end half an hour earlier.
   A. to be B. to have been C. being D. be
3. Time _____, the celebration will be held as scheduled.
   A. permit B. permitting C. permitted D. permits
4. Orangutans are said _____ the smallest animals compared with human beings.
   A. being B. to be C. to have been D. having been
5. It is difficult for a foreigner _____ Chinese.
   A. leaning B. being learned C. to be learned D. to learn
6. There are only ten apples left in the baskets, _____ the spoilt ones.
   A. not counting B. not to count
   C. don't count D. having not counted
7. I don't remember _____ a chance to try this method.
   A. to have been given B. to be given
   C. giving D. having been given
8. What a nice day! How about the three of us _____ a walk in the park nearby?
   A. to take B. take C. taking D. to be taking
9. _____ should not become a serious disadvantage in life and work.
   A. To be not tall B. Not being tall C. Being not tall D. Not to be tall
10. Sandy could do nothing but _____ his teacher that he was wrong.
    A. admit B. admitted C. admitting D. to admit

Section B Practical Writing

Applications for Scholarships or Assistantship
（申请奖学金和助学金）

Writing Tips

申请信要简单明了，分为开场白（Opener）、正文（Body）和结尾（Close）三部分，开场白不用客套话，应该开门见山，说明写信原因、兴趣等。其格式与普通书信格式一样，需有事由标题、信头日期、信内地址（封内地址）、称呼、正文、结尾客套语（敬语）、签名等。

申请信的类型：

（1）申请奖学金和助学金（Applications for Scholarships or Assistantship）。

（2）求职信（Applications for Job）。

（3）申请调动工作（Application for Transferring Post）。

（4）申请辞职（Application for Resignation）。

（5）申请报考国外大学（Applications for Going to College and University Abroad）。

(6)申请去国外大学攻读硕士学位(Applications for Going to University Abroad to Pursue Master's Degree)。

(7)申请护照和签证(Applications for Passport and Visa)。

(8)申请转换签证(Applications for Changing Passport and Visa)。

(9)申请出国进修(Applications for Advanced Studies Abroad)。

(10)申请做访问学者(Application for Being Visiting Learner)。

(11)申请参加学术会议(Applications for Taking Part in Academic Meeting)。

申请奖学金和助学金(Applications for Scholarships or Assistantship)应注意以下几点：

(1)写明申请学校和所学专业。

(2)提供申请人的个人经历。

(3)索取申请学校相关的申请表等。

(4)写申请时需要简明扼要。

申请奖学金和助学金的结构(Layout)：

(1)信头(Heading)：写信人的单位名称、地址、电话号码、传真、邮编和写信日期。信头的目的是让人立刻获得你隶属哪个学院、何时申请奖学金等信息，方便接收人回复。

(2)信内地址(Inside Address)：收信人的姓名、地址必须准确、具体。一般写在信头下面空一、两行处，信纸的左边，顶格写。

(3)称呼(Salutation)：不相识的男士/女士用 Dear Sir/Sirs(复)，Gentlemen(美式英语)，Dear Madam，相识的男士/女士用 Dear Mr. Luo，Dear Mrs. Zhang，Dear Miss Sun。

(4)正文(Body of Letter)。

(5)结尾客套语(Complimentary Close)。

(6)签名(Signature)。

(7)附件(Enclosures)。

寄发奖学金申请时，写信者需要随函附寄一些个人资料，如获奖证书、成绩单、身份证的复印件等，这些个人资料统称附件。两件以上 Enclosures，缩写为 Encls.，顶格写在署名下间隔一行处。

Sample

Dept. of Chemistry, Peking University
Beijing, 100081 P. R. China
Dec. 21, 2013

Dr. Francisco Gomes
Chairman, Department of Chemistry
University of Colorado at Denver
Denver, Colorado 80202

Dear Dr. Gomes,

    I have read the announcement regarding the scholarship in chemistry that the University of Colorado is offering. And I would like to submit my application. The enclosed application form for admission to the graduate school of your university will give my educational history. However, I would like to point out that I have just received an MSP.

Sincerely yours,
Ding Jian

Practical Tasks

Task You are required to write a Letter of Reservation according to the following instructions given in Chinese.

    假如你是即将毕业的李明,江西科技师范大学的学生,英语专业。你听老师说品行良好、成绩优秀的学生可以获得奖学金,你有意向申请此次奖学金,为此请书写一份申请书。

    要求:内容要提及你的专业水平优秀,申请原因。

    写信地址:江西科技师范大学596号,宿舍楼9栋。

    收信地址:江西科技师范大学学生管理中心。

    日期:7月15日。

    不能少于100词。

Module Ⅳ Leisure Time

Adele(阿黛尔)

Adele is a British. She was born in 1988 and grew up in the north of London.
She is a very young and famous singer. At the Grammy Award in 2009, she earned the Best New Artists and Best Female Pop Vocal Performance prizes.

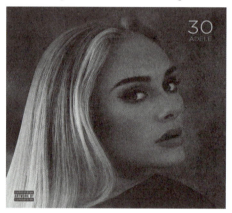

阿黛尔歌曲欣赏

Rolling in the Deep①

There's a fire starting in my heart
Reaching a fever pitch and it's bringing me out the dark
Finally I can see you crystal clear
Go ahead and sell me out and I'll lay your sheet bare
See how I leave with every piece of you
Don't underestimate the things that I will do
There's a fire starting in my heart
Reaching a fever pitch and it's bringing me out the dark
The scars of your love remind me of us
They keep me thinking that we almost had it all

---

① 此为歌词部分节选。

The scars of your love they leave me breathless
I can't help feeling
We could have had it all
Rolling in the Deep

UNIT 4

Travel

Unit 4　Travel

Learning Objectives

Students should be able to
★　Understand the dialogues and passage by listening.
★　Talk about different traveling places in China.
★　Master the new words and expressions.
★　Review Attributive Clause.
★　Learn how to write Resume.

Module Ⅰ　Listening

Task 1　Listen to the following conversations twice and choose the best answer to each question you hear in the recording.

1. A. Have a drink.　　　　　　　　B. Visit a company.
   C. Meet a friend.　　　　　　　　D. Write a report.
2. A. On television.　　　　　　　　B. Through the Internet.
   C. From a newspaper.　　　　　　D. Over the radio.
3. A. It snowed heavily.　　　　　　B. The wind was strong.
   C. It rained hard.　　　　　　　　D. The fog was thick.
4. A. In the city center.　　　　　　B. Away from the highway.
   C. Close to his office.　　　　　　D. Near the train station.
5. A. The man doesn't like the mobile phone.
   B. The man has bought a new mobile phone.
   C. The mobile phone has already been sold out.
   D. The mobile phone is too expensive for the man.

Task 2　Listen to the following passage twice and fill in the blanks with the missing words you hear in the recording.

　　There are about 3.7 million businesses in the UK. About 75% of British jobs are in ___6___ industries-hotels, restaurants, travel and shopping. These are the fastest ___7___ businesses and employ over twenty million people. Most British people work a five-day week. The working week is, ___8___, the longest of any country in Europe. In 1998 a new law ___9___. The law says that workers do not have to work more than 48 hours a week if they don't want to. According to the law, British employers must give their workers ___10___ of 24 days a year.

Module Ⅱ　Spotlight on Reading

Text A　Intensive Reading

Beautiful Mountain Wuyi

1　"The beauty of Mountain Wuyi will amaze you", my Chinese friends said when I would visit the nature **reserve** of Mountain Wuyi. While I was **impatient** to **verify** their comments. I was **skeptical**. As a Canadian I am **accustomed** to large acres of greenery and vast forest.

2　But now, I must confess my impression was wrong. I was not aware that a nature reserve could **embody** such splendid scenery and offer such startling **glimpse** of history and ancient culture in a country of 1.2 billion **inhabitants**. I have discovered the **marvel** of a nature coexisting in harmony and where modern life does not disrupt the rhythm of nature.

3　The reserve is divided into four zones for protection and conservation which offer unique characteristics: the conservation zone of the Jiuquxi River in the center, the natural and cultural zone in the east, and finally, the **ruins** of the **imperial** Minyue City of the Han Dynasty in the village of Chengcun. These zones formed a total environment which since 1987 has been recognized as part of the global network Man and Biosphere. To further promote preservation of this site, China has requested that Mountain Wuyi reserve be listed as a Natural and Cultural World **Heritage** site of UNESCO. (222 words)

Unit 4　Travel

New Words

reserve	/rɪˈzɜːv/	n. （野生动物）保护区
impatient	/ɪmˈpeɪʃ(ə)nt/	adj. 不耐烦的，没有耐心的
verify	/ˈverɪfaɪ/	v. 核实，查证
skeptical	/ˈskeptɪk(ə)l/	adj. 不相信的，持怀疑态度的
accustom	/əˈkʌstəm/	v. 使习惯于，使适应于
embody	/ɪmˈbɒdi/	v. 具体表现，体现
glimpse	/ɡlɪmps/	v. 瞥见；开始理解
inhabitant	/ɪnˈhæbɪtənt/	n. （某地的）居民
marvel	/ˈmɑːv(ə)l/	n. 令人惊异的人（或事），奇迹
ruin	/ˈruːɪn/	n. 遗迹，废墟
imperial	/ɪmˈpɪəriəl/	adj. 帝国的，皇帝的
heritage	/ˈherɪtɪdʒ/	n. 遗产

Phrases and Expressions

Jiuquxi River 九曲溪
Minyue City 闽越城
UNESCO 联合国教科文组织

Inquiry Learning

1. **I have discovered the marvel of a nature coexisting in harmony and where modern life does not disrupt the rhythm of nature.**
   我发现了自然和谐共存的奇迹,现代生活没有破坏自然的节奏。
   coexisting in harmony 作为后置定语修饰 nature。
   where 是定语从句中常用的关系副词,在从句中做地点状语,修饰 nature,引导定语从句。
2. **These zones formed a total environment which since 1987 has been recognized as part of the global network Man and Biosphere.**
   这些区域形成了一个整体的环境,自1987年以来一直被认为是人类和生物圈全球网络的一部分。
   Since 1987 是插入语, which 作为关系代词引导定语从句。

Reading Comprehension

Choose the best answer according to the passage.
1. What's the author's reaction after he heard that "the beauty of Mountain Wuyi will amaze you"? _____
   A. Eager to verify but doubtful.　　B. Eager to appreciate the beauty.
   C. Doubtful of its real beauty.　　　D. Indifferent and skeptical.
2. What does the word "confess" mean? _____
   A. Conclude.　　B. Confer.　　C. Accept.　　D. Consider.
3. According to the passage, what is the characteristic of Mountain Wuyi? _____
   A. Greenery and vast forests.　　B. Harmonious coexistence of man and nature.
   C. Splendid scenery.　　　　　　D. Rhythm of nature.
4. What's the zone in the west known for? _____
   A. Nature beauty.　　　　　　　B. Cultural diversity.
   C. Ecological conservation.　　　D. Conservation of biodiversity.
5. What attitude of the author towards Mountain Wuyi is concluded from this passage? _____
   A. Admiration.　　B. Negativity.　　C. Arrogance.　　D. Hostility.

Language in Use

Task 1 Find the right definition in Column B that matches the words in Column A.

Column A	Column B
1. verify	A. denying or questioning the tenets of especially a religion
2. imperial	B. a brief or incomplete view

3. skeptical   C. relating to or associated with an empire
4. glimpse   D. to check that something is true or accurate
5. embody   E. a person or an animal that lives in a particular place
6. inhabitant   F. to express or represent an idea or a quality

Task 2 Fill in the blank with the given words or expressions. Change the form where necessary.

| accustom | reserve | verify | embody | impatient | heritage |

1. The building is part of our national _____.
2. Some are so _____ to pigging out, they can't cut back.
3. You must _____ your strength for the tennis final.
4. As time went on, he grew more and more _____.
5. They take great pride in their _____.
6. It will take about six weeks to _____ the record with Guinness World Records.

Translation

Task 1 Translate the following sentences from Chinese into English with the phrases given in the brackets.

1. 她习惯每天早起锻炼(be accustomed to)
   _____

2. 我瞥了一眼她的书本。(a glimpse of)
   _____

3. 人们总是对于未知的事物充满怀疑。(skeptical)
   _____

4. 游客们看到古遗址赞叹不已。(heritage)
   _____

5. 他们的教育方式体现了学生的重要性。(embody)
   _____

Task 2 Translate the following sentences from English into Chinese.

1. Red represents happiness, luck and fortune while yellow symbolizes imperial holiness and dignity.
   _____

2. Vigorously improve forest inhabitant people's livelihood.
   _____

3. If you're still skeptical about exercising, we can only ask you to trust us and give it a try.
   _____

4. A large number of buildings fell into ruin after the revolution.

5. Please verify that there is sufficient memory available before loading the program.

Text B   Extensive Reading

Living in Hangzhou

1   I always think of Hangzhou as a big little city: big enough to be interesting; little enough to be friendly. I moved here four and a half years ago, after spending my childhood in rural Malaysia, and my early adulthood in the small town of Thailand. I have to say I've never felt more at home anywhere.

2   One of the best things about Hangzhou is how cheap it is: you can buy a delicious lunch for $4; rent a three-bedroom house for $800 a month; and at least every other shop is an antique or **thrift** store. With everything being so **affordable**, creativity and sub-culture **thrive** here. Hangzhou is a place where you can find a community of **vegans** or fat activists. Artists, musicians, and filmmakers can all meet like-minded souls. It's proved the perfect place for me and all my **punk** friends, and lately it's been so busy that people have started to call it the center of E-commerce in China.

3   There's been an amazing music scene here for decades—the traditional and modern have all been based in Hangzhou. But even though it's growing, the music scene is pretty close and friendly. A couple of years back, for instance, I needed **emergency gall bladder surgery** and Hangzhou band the Fireweed played a benefit show to raise money for it, which was lucky, since I had no money.

4   If you're an outdoor type, there's a lot to do. We're not far from nearby mountains. There's also West Lake downtown, where you can go **hiking**. Unfortunately, I hate the crowd of people! Heading west of downtown there's Forest Park for hiking, and we're also only two hours away from the sea Hangzhou Bay. There you can rent a tent and camp on the beach, which is something **outdoorsy** that I am actually **keen** to do. (324 words)

Unit 4 Travel

New Words

thrift	/θrɪft/	n. 节约,节俭
affordable	/əˈfɔːdəb(ə)l/	adj. 便宜的,付得起的
thrive	/θraɪv/	v. 茁壮成长,兴旺
feminist	/ˈfemənɪst/	n. 女权主义者
vegan	/ˈviːgən/	n. 纯素食者,严格的素食主义者
punk	/pʌnk/	n. 朋克;摇滚乐迷
emergency	/ɪˈmɜːdʒənsi/	n. 突发事件,紧急情况
gall	/gɔːl/	n. 胆汁;五倍子
bladder	/ˈblædə(r)/	n. 膀胱
surgery	/ˈsɜːdʒəri/	n. 外科手术
outdoorsy	/aʊtˈdɔːzi/	adj. 户外的,爱好野外活动的
keen	/kiːn/	adj. 渴望的,热衷的

Phrases and Expressions

feel at home 感到舒适,自在
far from... 远离……
Malaysia 马来西亚

Inquiry Learning

1. **Hangzhou is a place where you can find a community of vegans or fat activists.** 在杭州,你可以找到素食主义者或肥胖活动家的社区。
   where 作为关系副词引导定语从句。

2. **It's proved the perfect place for me and all my punk friends, and lately it's been so

busy that people have started to call it the center of E-commerce in China.**
事实证明,对我和我所有年少无知的朋友来说,它是一个完美的地方,最近这里如此繁忙,以至于人们开始称它为中国的电子商务中心。

so. . . that. . . 如此……以至于……

如:The city is so charming that many tourists come here.

这个城市如此迷人,以至于许多游客来这里。

3. **There's also West Lake downtown, where you can go hiking.**

市中心还有西湖,你可以去那里远足。

本句包含了一个由 where 引导的非限制性定语从句。

如:You can go to the library, where your classmates study together.

你可以去图书馆,在那里你的同学们一起学习。

4. **There you can rent a tent and camp on the beach, which is something outdoorsy that I am actually keen to do.**

在那里你可以租一个帐篷,在海滩上露营,这是我非常喜欢的户外活动。

本句中 which 引导了一个非限制性定语从句,整个从句修饰主句部分。

如:She was not herself today, which made her so inactive.

她今天身体不舒服,所以很不活跃。

Reading Comprehension

Choose the best answer according to the passage.

1. According to the passage, we can know that how long does the author live at Hangzhou? _____

    A. It was four and a half years.　　B. Since she was born.

    C. Since she was four and half years.　　D. It was a couple of years.

2. The author thinks of Hangzhou as _____.

    A. the center of E-commerce in China

    B. the most beautiful city in China

    C. big enough to be interesting; little enough to be friendly

    D. a creative and enough big city in the world

3. According to the passage, the author inferred that _____.

    A. Hangzhou is the most comfortable place for her

    B. Hangzhou is the best place for foreign tourists

    C. Hangzhou is a good place for online commerce

    D. Hangzhou is the place where she will have her rest life there

4. In the passage, people in the Hangzhou are productive and are eager to participate in _____.

    A. tourism　　B. politics　　C. foreign trade　　D. business

5. According to the passage, what's the best attitude of the author towards Hangzhou? _____

   A. Arrogant attitude.　　　　　　B. Positive attitude.
   C. Negative attitude.　　　　　　D. Selfish attitude.

Module Ⅲ　Building up More Skills

Section A　Grammar Tips

The Attributive Clause（定语从句）

英语句子中用来修饰名词、代词或句子的从句叫作定语从句（Attributive Clause）。定语从句在句中的作用相当于形容词，因此也被称为形容词关系代词性从句。它可以用来修饰名词或代词，也可用来修饰句中的某个短语，甚至整个句子。被定语从句修饰的词称为先行词（Antecedent）。引导定语从句的词被称为关系词（Relative Pronoun），它包括关系代词 that，who，whom，whose，which，as 等和关系副词（Relative Adverb）when，where，why 两种。

关系词	例词	所修饰的先行词	在从句中所做的成分	例句
关系代词	who	人	主语，宾语（可省略）	He has two daughters who study in the same college.
	whom	人	宾语（可省略）	She met the doctor whom she knew at her school.
	which	物	主语，宾语（可省略）	I like playing basketball which is my favorite sport.
	that	人或物	主语，宾语（可省略），表语	The book that is expensive is from my father.
	whose	人或物	定语	They live in a house whose decoration imitates Italian style.

关系词	例词	所修饰的先行词	在从句中所做的成分	例句
关系副词	**when**	时间名词	时间状语	Do you know the date when your mother was born?
	where	地点名词	地点状语	I know a place where it is greenery and around with mountains.
	why	原因名词	原因状语	There is no reason why he refused to our plan.

定语从句按照其与先行词的关系分为限制性定语从句和非限制性定语从句。

(1)对先行词起修饰、限制与确定的作用,若是去掉它,先行词便不能明确表示所指对象,是为限制性定语从句。

如:People who take physical exercise live longer.

进行体育锻炼的人活得长些。(若把从句去掉,句子就失去意义。)

His daughter, who is in Boston now, is coming home next week.

他女儿现在在波士顿,下星期回来。(若把从句去掉,句子意义仍然完整。)

(2)非限制性定语从句对先行词或主句起补充说明的作用,即使省去也不影响主句的语义完整性。非限制性定语从句与先行词或主句之间常用逗号隔开。非限制性定语从句关系代词有 who、whom、whose、which,没有 that。所有关系代词和关系副词均可引导限制性定语从句,大多数关系代词和关系副词可引导非限制性定语从句,但 that 不可。

如:We'll graduate in July, when we will be free.

我们将于七月份毕业,到那时我们就自由了。

Last week we travelled to Beijing, where there are many places of interest.

我们上周去了北京旅游,那儿有很多名胜古迹。

(3)非限制性定语从句与限制性定语从句的翻译不同。在翻译定语从句时,一般把限定性定语从句翻译在它所修饰的先行词之前,而把非限定性定语从句与主句分开。

如:He is the man whose car was stolen. 他就是汽车被窃的那个人。

I've invited Jim, who lives in the next flat. 我邀请了吉姆,他就住在隔壁。

(4)注意事项:关系代词 whom 在限制性定语从句中做宾语时可用 who 代替 whom,但 whom 在非限制性定语从句中做宾语时不可用 who 来代替。

如:This is the girl whom I met in the street.

这是我在街上遇到的那个女孩。

先行词 the girl 在限制性定语从句中做宾语,可用 who 代替 whom。

如:The woman, whom you met at my home, was a teacher.

你在我家遇到的那个女人是一个老师。

先行词 the woman 在非限制性定语从句中做宾语,不可用 who 代替 whom。

Unit 4 Travel

Practical Tasks

Task 1 Fill in the blanks with the correct answer.

1. As a child, Jack studied in a village school, _____ is named after his grandfather.
   A. which   B. where   C. what   D. that
2. The girl arranged to have piano lessons at the training center with her sister _____ she would stay for an hour.
   A. where   B. who   C. which   D. what
3. The settlement is home to nearly 1,000 people, many of _____ left their village homes for a better life in the city.
   A. whom   B. which   C. them   D. those
4. The old temple _____ roof was damaged in storm is now under repair.
   A. where   B. which   C. its   D. whose
5. That's the new machine _____ parts are too small to be seen.
   A. that   B. which   C. whose   D. what
6. After graduating from college, I took some time off to go traveling, _____ turned out to be a wise decision.
   A. that   B. which   C. when   D. where
7. I've become good friends with several of the students in my school _____ I met in the English speech contest last year.
   A. who   B. where   C. when   D. which
8. I refuse to accept the blame for something _____ was someone else's fault.
   A. who   B. that   C. as   D. what
9. Children who are not active or _____ diet is high in fat will gain weight quickly.
   A. what   B. whose   C. which   D. that
10. In China, the number of cities is increasing _____ development is recognized across the world.
    A. where   B. which   C. whose   D. what
11. This is the very letter _____ came last night.
    A. who   B. which   C. that   D. as
12. I know only a little about this matter; you may ask _____ knows better than I.
    A. whoever   B. whomever   C. anyone   D. the one
13. This is the school _____ we visited three days ago.
    A. where   B. /   C. when   D. what
14. This is the factory _____ we worked a year ago.
    A. where   B. that   C. which   D. on which
15. The foreign guests, _____ were government officials, were warmly welcomed at the airport.
    A. most of them   B. most of that   C. most of whom   D. most of those

Task 2 Fill in an appropriate relative pronoun or adverb for each blanks.

1. Sorry, we don't have the coat _____ you need.
2. This is the dictionary _____ Mum gave me for my birthday.
3. Do you know the man _____ is sitting behind Nancy?
4. I have found some pictures of the most interesting places _____ you can visit during the winter holidays.
5. I'd like to tell you about the table manners _____ you should know when you visit Korea.

Section B Practical Writing

个人简历(Resume)

Writing Tips

英语个人简历一般包括姓名、地址、年龄、学历、个人经历等内容。其没有固定的格式,由于使用目的不同,个人简历可以突出不同的内容,或增减部分内容。

一、个人资料(Personal Data)

    1. Sex 性别：Male 男,Female 女

    2. Family/Marital Status 婚姻状况：Single 单身, Unmarried 未婚, Married 已婚 Divorced 离异

    3. Date of Birth 出生年月

    4. Permanent/Temporary Address 永久(临时)住址

二、受教育情况(Educational Background)

    1. Have a thorough knowledge of the English language.

    2. In 2004, I graduated from Department of Mechanical Engineering at Nanchang University.

三、工作经历(Work Experience)

    1. Two years of secretary to the general manager

    2. Good at PC computer

    3. Proficient in English speaking and writing

四、申请目的(Objective)

    1. Preferring a job with greater challenges.

    2. Looking for a post with more chances to get promotion.

    3. Maximizing my advertising, designing and research skills in both print and media.

五、兴趣或爱好(Interests or Hobbies)

    Singing, dancing, playing the piano, surfing on the Internet and so on.

Sample

Name	Yang Jun
Address	Room 520
	No. 110 Xinhua Road
	Beijing 100011
	Tel：010-68506762
Personal Data	Date of Birth：August 20, 1994
	Nationality：Chinese
	Marital Status：Single
	Health：Excellent
	Sex：Female
Work Experience	2016—2019：Secretary to the General Manager in Changcheng Hotel, Beijing
Education	2013—2016：Beijing Zhongshan Vocational School
	2010—2013：Beijing Jingshan High School
	2007—2010：Beijing No. 40 Middle School
Interests	Singing, dancing, playing basketball, running

Practical Task

Please write a resume about yourself.

假如你是李明，你准备应聘一家网络公司的人事经理。你毕业于北京大学，工商管理专业，有过一年经历工作，目前单身。家住江西省南昌市红谷滩新区，现在要求做一份求职简历。

要求：字数不限，关于电话以及兴趣爱好可以自编，格式不限，内容简单明了。

Resume

Module Ⅳ Leisure Time

English Poetry Appreciation
Sonnet 18
William Shakespeare

Shall I compare thee to a summer's day?
我能否将你比作夏天?
Thou art more lovely and more temperate:
你比夏天更美丽温婉。
Rough winds do shake the darling buds of May,
狂风将五月的蓓蕾凋残,
And summer's lease hath all too short a date:
夏日的勾留何其短暂。
Sometime too hot the eye of heaven shines,
休恋那丽日当空,
And often is his gold complexion dimm'd;
转眼会云雾迷蒙。
And every fair from fair sometime declines,
休叹那百花飘零,
By chance or nature's changing course untrimm'd
催折于无常的天命。
But thy eternal summer shall not fade
唯有你永恒的夏日常新,
Nor lose possession of that fair thou owest;
你的美貌亦毫发无损。
Nor shall Death brag thou wander'st in his shade,
死神也无缘将你幽禁,
When in eternal lines to time thou growest:
你在我永恒的诗中长存。
So long as men can breathe or eyes can see,
只要世间尚有人吟诵我的诗篇,
So long lives this and this gives life to thee.
这诗就将不朽,永葆你的芳颜。

Unit 4　Travel

UNIT 5

Economy

Unit 5 Economy

Learning Objectives

Students should be able to
★ Understand the dialogues and passage by listening.
★ Talk about economy in daily life and know its definition.
★ Master the new words and expressions.
★ Review Attributive Clause.
★ Learn how to write the Letter of Application.

Module Ⅰ Listening

Task 1 Listen to the following conversations twice and choose the best answer to each question you hear in the recording.

1. A. Buy a gift.   B. Send a parcel.
   C. Book a ticket.   D. Rent an apartment.
2. A. He missed the bus.   B. He got lost.
   C. His car broke down.   D. His bicycle was stolen.
3. A. Buy the new software.   B. Ask Jack for help.
   C. Stop using the software.   D. Help the woman.
4. A. He is the new manager.   B. He is away on business.
   C. He is on sick leave.   D. He is retired.
5. A. Ask his parents for help.   B. Start to save money.
   C. Borrow money from his friends.   D. Get a loan from the bank.

Task 2 Listen to the following passage twice and fill in the blanks with the missing words you hear in the recording.

　　Ladies and gentlemen, good afternoon. First of all, let me ___6___ to you for coming to the opening ceremony of our new branch office.

　　This branch is the 25th office we have ___7___ so far. We are very happy that we have finally opened a branch in this city. This branch, we believe, will help ___8___ the local economy. And our company will in turn benefit from doing business here. We promise that we will provide the ___9___ to our customers. And, of course, we need your ___10___ and cooperation.

Module Ⅱ Spotlight on Reading

Text A Intensive Reading

The Booming "Lazy Economy" in China

1   A few days ago, "lazy **consumption** data" released by Taobao showed that in 2018, Chinese people spent 16 billion yuan on laziness, an increase of 70 percent compared with last year. Among them, **expenditures** by the post-1995 generation have increased the fastest, at 82 percent. Experts have pointed out that in the context of consumption upgrades, the "lazy economy" will usher in a new round of outbreaks.

Booming "O2O" business model

2   Behind this data is the online-to-offline business model, also known in its lazier version as "O2O" commerce. In it, companies offer consumers the ability to order online products to enhance their offline experiences—covering nearly every aspect of life.

Lazy products are most popular

3   We opened various e-commerce **platforms** and searched for "lazy products" as keywords. There were thousands of **commodity** records. Lazy drink caps, lazy brushing devices, lazy mops... Many products enhance the practical performance of goods and meet the needs of people who want to save time and effort.

Hot-selling products online

4   Lazy food is also popular with young people. We found on the Taobao platform that the highest monthly sales volume of the "**self-heating** hot pot", a big internet hit, is more than 400,000. At same time, other major brands including the instant noodle maker Tongyi, Haidilao catering, and snack giants Baicaowei and Bestore are also pushing the trend to launch similar products.

Different **characteristics** of different consumer preferences

5   From the **perspective** of consumer preferences, lazy consumers on Taobao have their own characteristics. Due to various needs that arise from laziness, various groups of "special consumers" have **emerged**, such as "The **Recliners**" "The Bending **Impaired**" and "The Housekeeping Experts". There are regional and age differences between different consumer groups, too.

6   The main **driver** behind the lazy economy is essentially consumers who have strong spending power and dare to try out different products and services. (308 words)

Unit 5　Economy

New Words

consumption	/kənˈsʌmpʃ(ə)n/	n. 消费,消耗
expenditure	/ɪkˈspendɪtʃə(r)/	n. 经费,支出额
boom	/buːm/	n. 繁荣　v. 迅速发展
platform	/ˈplætfɔːm/	n. 平台;讲台
commodity	/kəˈmɒdəti/	n. 商品,货物
self-heating	/self ˈhiːtɪŋ/	n. 自动加热
trend	/trend/	n. 趋势
launch	/lɔːntʃ/	v. 发动,发起
characteristic	/kærəktəˈrɪstɪk/	n. 特征,特点
perspective	/pəˈspektɪv/	n. （观察问题的）视角
emerge	/ɪˈmɜːdʒ/	v. 浮现,出现
recliner	/rɪˈklaɪnə(r)/	n. 斜靠着的人;躺着的人
impair	/ɪmˈpeə/	adj. 受损的
driver	/ˈdraɪvə(r)/	n. 推动力

Phrases and Expressions

in the context of... 在……情况下，在……背景下
arise from... 由……引起，起因
try out 试验
Tongyi 统一品牌
Baicaowei 百草味
Bestore 良品铺子

Inquiry Learning

1. **Experts have pointed out that in the context of consumption upgrades, the "lazy economy" will usher in a new round of outbreaks.**

   有专家指出,在消费升级的大背景下,"懒经济"将迎来新一轮爆发。

   point out 指出,that 后面引导宾语从句"the 'lazy economy' will usher in a new round of outbreaks"。

   "in the context of consumption upgrades"是插入语,做状语。

2. **Behind this data is the online-to-offline business model, also known in its lazier version as "O2O" commerce.**

   这些数据的背后是线上到线下的商业模式,也被称懒惰版本"O2O"商业。

   "known in its lazier version as 'O2O' commerce"作为非谓语动词,表示伴随。

3. **The Recliners 躺椅族**

   It means a group of people who lie down all the time and live a colorful life with their smartphones.

   一群整天躺着,用智能手机过着丰富多彩的生活的人。

4. **The Bending Impaired 弯曲障碍族**

   It means people who regard bending as the enemy, and use lazy products to avoid doing things such as tying shoelaces. 他们视弯曲为敌人,使用懒人产品来避免做系鞋带等事情。

5. **The Housekeeping Experts 家政专家族**

   It means people who are good at commanding high-tech electronic products like sweeping robots to help solve family problems. "家政专家"擅长指挥扫地机器人等高科技电子产品,帮助其解决家庭问题。

Unit 5 Economy

Reading Comprehension

Choose the best answer according to the passage.

1. According to the passage, what's "lazy economic"? _____
   A. Lazy products.
   B. Lazy people earn money.
   C. Lazy consumptionon Taobao.
   D. Lazy expenditures online.
2. From the passage, the author mentioned many lazy commodities except _____.
   A. lazy drink caps
   B. lazy brushing devices
   C. lazy mops
   D. lazy makeup
3. Due to various needs arising from laziness, there are different groups of "special consumers" like _____.
   A. Housewife Experts
   B. The Bending Impaired
   C. Decliners
   D. Office Workers
4. What's the main driver behind the lazy economy? _____
   A. Consumers with spending power and accepting news products.
   B. Consumers with too much money and no time.
   C. Consumers with brevity to try new devices.
   D. Consumers with too much time and too much money.
5. What's best attitude of the author towards the lazy economy? _____
   A. Positive.   B. Negative.   C. Objective.   D. Active.

Language in Use

Task 1 Find the right definition in Column B that matches the words in ColumnA.

Column A	Column B
1. boom	A. the act of using energy, food or materials
2. consumption	B. a sudden increase in trade and economic activity
3. trend	C. to damage something or make something worse
4. impair	D. a general direction in which a situation is changing or developing
5. perspective	E. to start an activity, especially an organized one
6. launch	F. a way of thinking about something

Task 2　Fill in the blank with the given words or expressions. Change the form where necessary.

drive　　characteristic　　emerge　　commodity　　boom　　expenditure

1. Some animals possess the _____ of humans.
2. New things _____ day after day.
3. He is rigorous in his control of _____.
4. Crude oil is the world's most important _____.
5. An economic _____ followed, especially in housing and construction.
6. One _____ is a perception that the U. S. is doing better than other mature economies.

Translation

Task 1　Translate the following sentences from Chinese into English with the phrases given in the brackets.

1. 我们应该根据这一事件的前因后果寻求解决办法。(in the context of)

2. 他得以试用了所有的新软件。(try out)

3. 身体上的原因可以引起情绪或精神上的问题。(arise from)

4. 能源消耗随着各国工业化而增加。(consumption)

5. 从这个角度来看,失业问题将更加突出。(perspective)

Task 2　Translate the following sentences from English into Chinese.

1. These statistics display a definite trend.

3. An estimated 19 million children are visually impaired.

3. Living standards improved rapidly during the post-war boom.

4. I sat in my father's chair, a mustard-coloured recliner.

5. She used the newspaper column as a platform for her feminist views.

Unit 5　Economy

Text B　Extensive Reading

Economics

1　You may not read the **financial** pages of the newspaper, but you make **economic** choices every day. Each time you spend, save, or earn money, you are participating in the economy.

2　Economics is the study of how people use limited resources to produce, **distribute**, and **consume** goods and services. Goods are products that can be seen and touched. Services are work done for someone else. Let's say that you **deliver** newspapers door-to-door every morning before school. The newspapers are goods. In delivering them to consumers, you are providing a service.

3　The simple act of delivering newspapers leads to several economic questions. How much does it cost to produce the papers? What price will consumers pay for them? How much will you be paid for delivering them?

4　Many factors affect prices, but **supply** and **demand** top the list. When supply is greater than demand, prices tend to drop. When demand is higher than supply, prices tend to rise.

5　Let's say that you want to **bake** chocolate-chip cookies. You prepare a list of the **ingredients** that will be needed and go to the supermarket. When you reach for the **vanilla** extract, you gasp: $5.99 for a two-ounce bottle! The last time you bought the spice, it cost about $3. What made the price double?

6　That little bottle you're holding contains a product made from vanilla beans. The African country of Madagascar produces more than half the world's supply of vanilla. A few years ago, a major storm destroyed many of Madagascar's vanilla farms. Then, some **turmoil** there disrupted shipping. Those problems reduced the supply of vanilla beans. Yet demand remained the same. The scarcity of beans caused the price of products dependent on them to rise.

7　But conditions change. The high prices **tempted** more Madagascan farmers to grow vanilla. This year's crop may be the largest ever. The oversupply will probably lower vanilla prices.

8　Consumers may be willing to pay more for things they really want. If a price is set too high, though, many people may refuse to buy a product. If it is set too low, the company won't be able to stay in business. (362 words)

New Words

financial	/faɪˈnænʃ(ə)l/	adj.	财政的,金融的
economic	/ˌiːkəˈnɒmɪk/	adj.	经济的,经济学的
distribute	/dɪˈstrɪbjuːt/	v.	分发,分配
consume	/kənˈsjuːm/	v.	消耗,消费
deliver	/dɪˈlɪvə(r)/	v.	投递,运送
supply	/səˈplaɪ/	n. 供给量 v. 供应
demand	/dɪˈmɑːnd/	n.	需求
bake	/beɪk/	v.	烤,烘
ingredient	/ɪnˈɡriːdiənt/	n.	(食品的)成分,原料
vanilla	/vəˈnɪlə/	n.	香草精
turmoil	/ˈtɜːmɔɪl/	n. 混乱,骚乱 v. 扰乱
tempt	/tempt/	v.	引诱,诱惑

Phrases and Expressions

African 非洲的
Madagascar 马达加斯加岛
participate in 参与
lead to 导致

Inquiry Learning

Economics is the study of how people use limited resources to produce, distribute, and consume goods and services.
经济学是研究人们如何利用有限的资源生产、分配和消费商品和服务的学科。

本句中"how people use limited resources to produce, distribute, and consume goods and services"一起作为介词 of 的宾语,表明上文 study 的对象。

如:The professor is studying of how to make more functions for their products.

教授正在研究如何使他们的产品具有更多的功能。

Reading Comprehension

Choose the best answer according to the passage.

1. According to the passage, what is the economics? _____
    A. The study of the supply and demand of people.
    B. The study of how people to consume goods.
    C. The study to learn how people sell good to other people.
    D. The study to learn how people use limited resources to produce, distribute, and consume goods and services.
2. In the passage, what is the main factors to affect prices _____.
    A. the quality of goods   B. the brand of goods
    C. the preference of people   D. the supply and demand
3. In the passage, what reasons lead to the reduction the supply of vanilla beans? _____
    A. A major storm and some turmoil.   B. The bad weather and some turmoil.
    C. People's less demand.   D. No people to cultivate vanilla beans.
4. From the paragraph six, what the meaning of the word "scarcity"? _____
    A. Shortage.   B. Precious.   C. Enough.   D. Valuable.
5. According to the whole passage, we can know whether consumer buy goods or not depends on _____.
    A. price   B. quality
    C. price and preference D. quality and price

Module Ⅲ Building up More Skills

Section A Grammar Tips

The Attributive Clause(定语从句)

1. that 和 which 引导定语从句的区别

(1)替代作用不同。that 在从句中既可指人,也可指物,而 which 在从句中只可指物,不可指人。

（2）适用从句类型不同。that 与 which 均可引导限制性定语从句，但 which 还可引导非限制性定语从句，并且 which 也可以用作介词宾语，构成"介词+关系代词 which"的结构。

（3）词性不同。that 与 which 均可用作关系代词，在定语从句中充当主语或宾语，充当宾语时均可省略，但 that 还可用作关系副词，在定语从句中充当状语。

（4）在下列情况下，只用 that 不用 which。

①当先行词是不定代词 all, little, few, much, anything, everything, nothing, none, some 等时只用 that。

Do you have anything that you want to say for yourself?

你还有什么想要为你自己说的吗？

②先行词被 all, every, no, some, any, little, much, the only, the very, the right, the last, few, just 等修饰时只用 that。

This is the very person that I'm waiting for.

这正是我在等的人。

③有最高级修饰或者先行词本身就是序数词或形容词最高级时只用 that。

The first book that I bought is about how to study English well.

我买的第一本书是关于如何学好英语的。

④当先行词既有人又有物时只用 that。

Do you know the things and persons that they are talking about?

你知道他们正在谈论的人和事吗？

⑤当主句的主语是疑问词 who 或 which 时只用 that。

Which is the bike that you lost?

哪一辆是你丢的自行车？

⑥当先行词在主句中做表语，而关系代词在从句中也做表语时，只用 that。

Shanghai is no longer the city that it used to be.

上海不再是过去的上海了。

⑦以 here/there 开头的句子只用 that。

Here is a hotel that you've been looking for.

这就是你一直在找的旅馆。

⑧句子中有两个定语从句时，其中一个已用关系代词 which，另外一个则用 that，反之亦然。

They secretly built up a small factory, which produced things that could cause pollution.

他们秘密地建起了一个小工厂，这个工厂生产的产品会引起污染。

2. 介词+which/whom 引导的定语从句

"介词+which"可以替代 when, where, why 等；"介词+whom"在定语从句中没有与之对应的替代词。

（1）替代 when。

I'll never forget the days on which (when) we studied together.

我永远忘不了我们一起学习的日子。

（2）替代 where。

This is the town in which (where) Shakespeare was born.

这就是莎士比亚出生的城镇。

（3）替代 why。

There's no reason for which (why) we shouldn't be friends.

我们没有理由不能成为朋友。

（4）替代 that。

There are varieties of ways in which (that) we can solve this problem.

我们有很多方法可以解决这个问题。

（5）"名词/代词+介词+关系代词"结构。

此类结构常见的有"some/several/a few/a little/many/more/most/the largest (land) + of+which/whom"等形式。

Here are the questions, some of which (= of which some) I thought difficult for you.

问题都在这儿，其中一些我认为对你来说太难。

（6）关系代词前介词的确定。

①依据定语从句中动词或形容词等所需要的某种习惯搭配来确定。

I bought a great many books, on which I spent all my money that I saved.

我买了很多书，这些书花了我积攒的所有钱。（依据 spend...on 确定）

②依据与先行词搭配的具体意义而定。

I'll never forget the time during which I spent my childhood in the country.

我从未忘记在那个乡村度过的少年时光。

Practical Tasks

Task 1　Fill in the blanks with the correct answer.

1. She had three sons, and all ＿＿＿＿＿ became doctors.
   A. who　　　　　　B. whose　　　　　　C. of them　　　　　　D. of whom
2. There are few places downtown for parking, ＿＿＿＿＿ is really a problem.
   A. which　　　　　B. what　　　　　　　C. it　　　　　　　　D. that
3. I can think of many cases ＿＿＿＿＿ students can't write a good article though having a large vocabulary.
   A. where　　　　　B. which　　　　　　C. that　　　　　　　D. to which
4. Living in the central Australian desert has its problems, ＿＿＿＿＿ obtaining water is not the least.
   A. of which　　　　B. for what　　　　　C. as　　　　　　　　D. whose
5. I have reached a point in my life ＿＿＿＿＿ I am supposed to make decisions of my own.
   A. which　　　　　B. where　　　　　　C. how　　　　　　　D. why
6. Barack Obama told millions ＿＿＿＿＿ him that his grandmother's influence on ＿＿＿＿＿ he is and the way he views the world was significant.
   A. watch; how　　　　　　　　　　　　B. watching; who

   C. watched; where   D. to watch; what

7. There is hardly an environment on earth _____ some species of animal or other have not adapted successfully.
  A. in which   B. on which   C. to which   D. for which

8. In fact, _____ many have pointed out over the years Dickens practically invented the way people celebrate Christmas in modern times.
  A. as   B. which   C. that   D. what

9. He changed his mind at the last minute, _____ made me very angry.
  A. when   B. that   C. which   D. it

10. A few people were killed in the fire, but _____ were saved.
  A. the most   B. most of them   C. most of whom   D. most

11. The man _____ visited our school yesterday is from London.
  A. who   B. which   C. whom   D. when

12. The woman _____ is talking to my mother is a friend of hers.
  A. whose   B. who   C. whom   D. which

13. Because of my poor memory. All _____ you told me has been forgotten.
  A. that   B. which   C. what   D. as

14. Do you remember those days _____ we spent along the seashore very happily?
  A. when   B. where   C. which   D. who

15. Tom did not take away the camera because it was just the same camera _____ he lost last week
  A. which   B. that   C. whom   D. as

Task 2 Fill in an appropriate relative pronoun or adverb for each blanks.

1. Do you know the girl _____ is standing under the tree?
2. I like to live in a house _____ is big and bright.
3. I hate people _____ talk much but do little.
4. Is the woman _____ talked to our teacher yesterday your mother?
5. The young lady _____ we met yesterday is our new math teacher.

Section B Practical Writing

A Letter of Application（求职信）

Writing Tips

  求职信是求职者写给用人单位的信，目的是让对方了解自己、相信自己、录用自己，它是一种私人对公并有求于公的信函。

  求职信的格式有一定的要求，内容要求简练、明确，切忌模糊、笼统、面面俱到。

一、常用句型(Useful Patterns)

1. 关于信息来源

  ①With reference to your advertisement in the Morning Post...

②I would like to apply for the post of Assistant Manager.

③I have seen your advertisement in the newspaper and I am interested in applying for the post of Secretary to the Sales Manager.

④I am interested in your advertisement for an Export Sales Manager.

⑤I should like to apply for the position of Sales Representative as advertised in yesterday's...

2. 描述经历

①As you can see from the enclosed curriculum vitae(履历表), I have had long experience in different fields.

②In my last job the administrative side was extremely important and I learnt to work under pressure.

③In my last job there was a lot of using computers.

④In my present job, public relations(人际关系) is a very important aspect and I run the office independently.

3. 选择新工作理由

①However, although I like my present job, I would now prefer a post offering more responsibility/chances of promotion.

②I'm happy in my present job. However, I am now looking for a post where I can use my knowledge of languages.

③I now feel I should like the greater challenge of managing a group of hotels.

④I'm delighted to have the possibility of employment with a company where I can use my financial knowledge.

Sample

Fenghou Road,
Fengcheng, Jiang
Tel: 0792-8262600
October 25, 2021

Dear Sir or Madam,

　　I'm writing in reply to your advertisement in *China Daily* of October 15 for an assistant to the Sales Manager. I am 24 years old, married with a daughter. I am at present secretary in the Johnson Paper Company. Having been in this position for four years, I am good at public relations. But I am now looking for a post where I can use my knowledge of business and marketing. My English is good: I have passed the English Band 6 Examination.

　　I hope I may be of interest to you, and I look forward to hearing from you.

Yours faithfully,
LIU Xin

Practical Tasks

You are required to write a letter of application according to the following instructions given in Chinese.

你是即将毕业的刘欣,一名计算机专业的学生。你偶然在网络上看到 Outstanding Software Company 招聘网络技术人员,你有意申请,为此请书写一封求职申请书。

要求:
1. 内容要提及你的专业水平优秀及求职原因。
2. 收信地址:江西省南昌市红谷滩 2888 号,日期:11 月 28 日。
3. 不少于 100 词。

Module Ⅳ Leisure Time

Auld Lang Syne
Keri Nobb

Should auld acquaintance be forgot
怎能忘记旧日朋友
And never brought to mind
心中能不怀想
Should auld acquaintance be forgot
旧日朋友岂能相忘
And auld lang syne
友谊地久天长
For auld lang syne my dear
为友谊地久天长,朋友

For auld lang syne
为友谊地久天长
We'll take a cup of kindness yet
让我们举杯痛饮
For auld lang syne
为友谊地久天长
We two have paddled in the stream
我们也曾终日逍遥
From morning sun till dine
从清晨直到日落
But seas between us broad have roared
如今却远隔重洋
Singing song lang syne
同声歌唱友谊地久天长
For auld lang syne my dear
为友谊地久天长,朋友
For auld lang syne
为友谊地久天长
We'll take a cup of kindness yet
现在让我们举杯痛饮
For auld lang syne
为友谊地久天长
And there's a hand my trusted friend
让我们亲密挽着手
And given a hand of day
情意永不相忘
We'll take a right good drunk
让我们来举杯畅饮
For auld lang syne
为友谊地久天长
For auld lang syne my dear
友谊地久天长,朋友
For auld lang syne
为友谊地久天长
We'll take a cup of kindness yet
现在让我们举杯痛饮
For auld lang syne
为友谊地久天长

Appendix A Vocabulary Index

A

ability /əˈbɪləti/	n. 能力	U1
access /ˈækses/	n. 入口 v. 接近	U1
achieve /əˈtʃiːv/	v. 获得,完成,达到	U1
advance /ədˈvɑːns/	v. (使)前进;发展	U1
advantage /ədˈvɑːntɪdʒ/	n. 有利条件,优势	U1
afraid /əˈfreɪd/	adj. 害怕的;担心的	U1
aim /eɪm/	n. 目标,目的	U1
allow /əˈlaʊ/	v. 允许,准许	U1
avoid /əˈvɔɪd/	v. 避免,防止	U1
a huge amount of 大量的		U1
auspicious /ɔːˈspɪʃəs/	adj. 吉兆的;吉利的	U2
affection /əˈfekʃən/	n. 喜爱;喜欢	U2
application /ˌæplɪˈkeɪʃ(ə)n/	n. 申请	U3
appear /əˈpɪə/	v. 出现,呈现	U3
accustom /əˈkʌstəm/	v. 使习惯于,使适应于	U4
affordable /əˈfɔːdəb(ə)l/	adj. 便宜的,付得起的	U4
arise from 由……引起,起因		U5
African 非洲的		U5

B

billion /ˈbɪljən/	num. 十亿	U1
be able to 能够		U1
be interested in... 对……感兴趣		U1
be hard on... 对……苛刻;对……要求严格		U1
bring into 使开始;使进入某种状态		U1
blessing /ˈblesɪŋ/	n. 祝福	U2
be bound to 肯定,注定		U2
boom /buːm/	n. 繁荣	U3
browse the web 浏览网页		U3

Appendix A Vocabulary Index

beware of... 对……谨慎 U3
build one's trust 建立信任 U3
bladder /ˈblædə(r)/ n. 膀胱 U4
bake /beɪk/ v. 烤, 烘 U5

C

chat /tʃæt/ v. 闲聊 U1
communicate /kəˈmjuːnɪkeɪt/ v. 交流, 传递信 U1
copy /ˈkɒpi/ n. 复印件, 副本 U1
cross off 从……划掉, 删除 U1
customary /ˈkʌstəməri/ adj. 照习惯法的; 照惯例的 U2
courageously /kəˈreɪdʒəsli/ adv. 勇敢地 U2
computerization /kəmˌpjutəraɪˈzeɪʃn/ n. 电脑化 U3
cyber /ˈsaɪbə/ adj. 与计算机有关的 U3
concern about... 对……担心 U3
contact /ˈkɒntækt/ v. 联系, 接触 U3
convincingly /kənˈvɪnsɪŋli/ adv. 令人信服地 U3
consumption /kənˈsʌmpʃ(ə)n/ n. 消费, 消耗 U5
commodity /kəˈmɒdəti/ n. 商品, 货物 U5
characteristic /kærəktəˈrɪstɪk/ n. 特征, 特点 U5
consume /kənˈsjuːm/ v. 消耗, 消费 U5

D

designate /ˈdezɪɡˌneɪt/ v. 选定; 指派 U2
deserve /dɪˈzɜːv/ v. 应受; 应得; 值得 U2
descend /dɪˈsend/ v. 下降; 下落; U2
dexterity /dekˈsterəti/ n. 灵巧; 机敏 U2
diversified /daɪˈvɜːsɪfaɪd/ adj. 多样化的; 多种多样的 U2
domestic /dəˈmestɪk/ adj. 家庭的; 国内的 U2
devote to 忠于; 致力于 U2
discover /dɪˈskʌvə/ v. 发现 U3
detail /ˈdiːteɪl/ n. 细节, 详情 U3
driver /ˈdraɪvə(r)/ n. 推动力 U5
distribute /dɪˈstrɪbjuːt/ v. 分发, 分配 U5
deliver /dɪˈlɪvə(r)/ v. 投递, 运送 U5
demand /dɪˈmɑːnd/ n. 需求 U5

E

education /ˌedʒuˈkeɪʃ(ə)n/ n. 教育	U1
entertainment /ˌentəˈteɪnmənt/ n. 娱乐	U1
excel /ɪkˈsel/ v. 精通,擅长	U1
economy /ɪˈkɒnəmi/ n. 经济;节约	U2
enthusiasm /ɪnˈθuːziæzəm/ n. 热情	U3
eventually /ɪˈventʃuəli/ adv. 最终	U3
exploit /ɪkˈsplɔɪt/ v. 利用,开发	U3
embody /ɪmˈbɒdi/ v. 具体表现,体现	U4
emergency /ɪˈmɜːdʒənsi/ n. 突发事件,紧急情况	U4
expenditure /ɪkˈspendɪtʃə(r)/ n. 经费,支出额	U5
emerge /ɪˈmɜːdʒ/ v. 浮现,出现	U5
economic /ˌiːkəˈnɒmɪk/ adj. 经济的,经济学的	U5

F

failure /ˈfeɪljə(r)/ n. 失败;失败的人	U1
folklore /ˈfəʊklɔː(r)/ n. 民间传说	U2
fairy /ˈfeəri/ n. 仙女;小精灵	U2
forcibly /ˈfɔːsəbli/ adv. 强行地;强烈地	U2
faithful /ˈfeɪθfəl/ adj. 忠诚的;忠实的;可靠的	U2
favor /ˈfeɪvə/ v. 比较喜欢,有利于,帮助	U3
fax /fæks/ n. 传真机	U3
flow of... ……的流动	U3
fake /feɪk/ adj. 伪造的,假货	U3
feminist /ˈfemənɪst/ n. 女权主义者	U4
feel at home 感到舒适,自在	U4
far from... 远离……	U4
financial /faɪˈnænʃ(ə)l/ adj. 财政的,金融的	U5

G

galaxy /ˈgæləksi/ n. 银河,星系	U2
gap /gæp/ n. 缝隙,缺口	U3
glimpse /glɪmps/ v. 瞥见;开始理解	U4
gall /gɔːl/ n. 胆汁;五倍子	U4

Appendix A Vocabulary Index

H

homonym /ˈhɒmənɪm/	n. 同音异义词；同形异义词	U2
hack /hæk/	v. 非法侵入	U3
heritage /ˈherɪtɪdʒ/	n. 遗产	U4

I

international /ˌɪntəˈnæʃ(ə)nəl/	adj. 国际的	U2
in effect 实际上		U2
immortal /ɪˈmɔːtl/	adj. 不朽的；流芳百世的	U2
income /ˈɪnkʌm/	n. 收入，收益	U3
in general 总之，通常		U3
imitate /ˈɪmɪteɪt/	v. 模仿，伪造	U3
ignorant /ˈɪɡnərənt/	adj. 无知的	U3
impatient /ɪmˈpeɪʃ(ə)nt/	adj. 不耐烦的，没有耐心的	U4
inhabitant /ɪnˈhæbɪtənt/	n.（某地的）居民	U4
imperial /ɪmˈpɪəriəl/	adj. 帝国的，皇帝的	U4
impair /ɪmˈpeə/	adj. 受损的	U5
ingredient /ɪnˈɡriːdiənt/	n.（食品的）成分，原料	U5
in the context of... 在……情况下，在……背景下		U5

K

keen /kiːn/	adj. 渴望的，热衷的	U4

L

longevity /lɒnˈdʒevəti/	n. 长命；长寿	U2
look forward to 期盼，期待		U2
location /ləʊˈkeɪʃən/	n. 地点，位置	U3
launch /lɔːntʃ/	v. 发动，发起	U5
lead to 导致		U5

M

move on 往前走，前进		U1

merge with 合并	U2
military /ˈmɪlətəri/ n. 军事,军方	U3
make use of 充分利用	U3
marvel /ˈmɑːv(ə)l/ n. 令人惊异的人(或事),奇迹	U4
Madagascar 马达加斯加岛	U5

N

natural /ˈnætʃ(ə)rəl/ adj. 天然的	U1
neutral /ˈnjuːtrəl/ adj. 中立的	U1

O

organize /ˈɔːɡənaɪz/ v. 组织	U1
original /əˈrɪdʒən(ə)l/ adj. 起初的,原先的	U1
overload /ˌəʊvəˈləʊd/ v. 超载,负担过重	U3
ownership /ˈəʊnəʃɪp/ n. 所有权	U3
offer /ˈɒfə/ v. 提供,报价	U3
online /ˈɒnlaɪn/ adj. 网上的,联机的	U3
over time 久而久之	U3
outdoorsy /aʊtˈdɔːzɪ/ adj. 户外的,爱好野外活动的	U4

P

pronounce /prəˈnaʊns/ v. 发(音),读(音)	U1
pavilion /pəˈvɪljən/ n. 阁楼	U2
pay attention to 注意,留心	U2
pursue /pəˈsjuː/ v. 追赶;追求	U2
poll /pəʊl/ n. 民意调查,选举投票	U3
private /ˈpraɪvət/ adj. 私人的,秘密的	U3
punk /pʌŋk/ n. 废物;年轻无知的人	U4
platform /ˈplætfɔːm/ n. 平台;讲台	U5
perspective /pəˈspektɪv/ n. (观察问题的)视角	U5
participate in 参与	U5

R

reduction /rɪˈdʌkʃ(ə)n/ n. 减小,降低	U1

Appendix A Vocabulary Index

refreshing /rɪˈfreʃɪŋ/   *adj.* 别有韵致的；给人新鲜感的   U2
refer to 提到，涉及   U2
register /ˈredʒɪstə/   *v.* 登记；注册   U2
race /reɪs/   *n.* 赛跑，人种，竞赛   U3
reassurance /ˌriːəˈʃʊrəns/   *v.* 保证，安慰   U3
relationship /rɪˈleɪʃ(ə)nʃɪp/   *n.* 关系，关联   U3
receive /rɪˈsiːv/   *v.* 收到，接待   U3
reserve /rɪˈzɜːv/   *n.* (野生动物)保护区   U4
ruin /ˈruːɪn/   *n.* 遗迹，废墟   U4
recliner /rɪˈklaɪnə(r)/   *n.* 斜靠着的人；躺着的人   U5

S

seriously /ˈsɪəriəsli/   *adv.* 严肃地，认真地   U1
service /ˈsɜːvɪs/   *n.* 服务   U1
step /step/   *v.* 跨步走，踏； *n.* 迈步，脚步   U1
stress /stres/   *n.* 精神压力，紧张   U1
success /səkˈses/   *n.* 成功，胜利   U1
stipulate /ˈstɪpjuleɪt/   *v.* 规定；约定   U2
scenery /ˈsiːnəri/   *n.* 风景；景色   U2
symbolic /sɪmˈbɒlɪk/   *adj.* 象征的；符号的   U2
separate /ˈsepərət/   *adj.* 单独的   U3
scam /skæm/   *v.* 诈骗   U3
suspicious /səˈspɪʃəs/   *adj.* 可疑的   U3
sincere /sɪnˈsɪr/   *adj.* 真诚的   U3
send /send/   *v.* 发送，派遣   U3
skeptical /ˈskeptɪk(ə)l/   *adj.* 不相信的，持怀疑态度的   U4
surgery /ˈsɜːdʒəri/   *n.* 外科手术   U4
self-heating /self ˈhiːtɪŋ/   *n.* 自动加热   U5
supply /səˈplaɪ/   *n.* 供给量 *v.* 供应   U5

T

tip /tɪp/   *n.* 诀窍，建议   U1
translate /trænzˈleɪt/   *v.* 翻译   U1
treat /triːt/   *v.* 对待，看待   U1
take away 带走；拿走   U1
try to do 尝试做某事   U1

trendy /ˈtrendi/	adj. 时髦的；赶时髦的	U2
thanks to 多亏了		U2
tear apart 分开，裂开		U2
trend /trend/	n. 趋势，热门话题	U3
trick /trɪk/	n. 花招，恶作剧，技巧	U3
thrift /θrɪft/	n. 节约，节俭	U4
thrive /θraɪv/	v. 茁壮成长，兴旺	U4
trend /trend/	n. 趋势	U5
turmoil /ˈtɜːmɔɪl/	n. 混乱，骚乱 v. 扰乱	U5
tempt /tempt/	v. 引诱，诱惑	U5
try out 试验		U5

U

usage /ˈjuːsɪdʒ/	n. 用法	U3

V

valuable /ˈvæljuəb(ə)l/	adj. 贵重的；有益的	U1
various /ˈveəriəs/	adj. 各种各样的	U1
version /ˈvɜːrʒn/	n. 版本；译文	U2
verify /ˈverɪfaɪ/	v. 核实，查证	U4
vegan /ˈviːgən/	n. 纯素食者，严格的素食主义者	U4
vanilla /vəˈnɪlə/	n. 香草精	U5

W

why not 为什么不		U1
weave /wiːv/	v. 编织；纺织	U2
worship /ˈwɜːʃɪp/	v. 崇拜；爱慕	U2

Appendix B Irregular Verbs

Infinitive	Past Tense	Past Participle	Explanation
arise	arose	arisen	出现
awake	awoke	awoken	唤醒
be	was, were	been	是
beat	beat	beaten	击打
become	became	become	变成
begin	began	begun	开始
bend	bent	bent	鞠躬
bet	bet	bet	打赌
bid	bade, bid	bidden, bid	出价
bind	bound	bound	绑
bite	bit	bitten	咬
bleed	bled	bled	流血
bless	blest, blessed	blest, blessed	祝福
blow	blew	blown	吹
break	broke	broken	断开
bring	brought	brought	带来
build	built	built	建筑
burn	burnt, burned	burnt, burned	燃烧
burst	burst	burst	爆炸
buy	bought	bought	买
catch	caught	caught	抓住
choose	chose	chosen	选择
come	came	come	来
cost	cost	cost	价值
cut	cut	cut	切
dare	dared	dared	敢
deal	dealt	dealt	处理
dig	dug	dug	挖
do	did	done	做
draw	drew	drawn	画
dream	dreamed, dreamt	dreamed, dreamt	做梦

Infinitive	Past Tense	Past Participle	Explanation
drink	drank	drunk	喝
drive	drove	driven	驾车
fall	fell	fallen	落下
feed	fed	fed	喂
fight	fought	fought	打架
find	found	found	找寻
fly	flew	flown	飞
forbid	forbad	forbidden	禁止
forecast	forecast, forecasted	forecast, forecasted	预报
forget	forgot	forgotten, forgot	忘记
forgive	forgave	forgiven	原谅
freeze	froze	frozen	冷冻
give	gave	given	给予
grave	graved	graven, graved	铭记
grow	grew	grown	成长
have	had	had	有
hear	heard	heard	听
hide	hid	hidden	隐藏
hit	hit	hit	打
hold	held	held	拿住
hurt	hurt	hurt	伤害
keep	kept	kept	保持
knit	knitted, knit	knitted, knit	编,织
know	knew	known	知道
lay	laid	laid	放置
lead	led	led	带领
lean	leaned, leant	leaned, leant	倾斜
learn	learnt, learned	learnt, learned	学习
leave	left	left	离开
lend	lent	lent	借出
lie	lay	lain	躺下
	lied	lied	撒谎
light	lit	lit	点燃
	lighted	lighted	照亮
lose	lost	lost	丢失
make	made	made	做

Appendix B Irregular Verbs

Infinitive	Past Tense	Past Participle	Explanation
mean	meant	meant	意思
meet	met	met	见面
misgive	misgave	misgiven	担忧
mislead	misled	misled	误导
mistake	mistook	mistaken	弄错
misunderstand	misunderstood	misunderstood	误会
outdo	outdid	outdone	胜过
outeat	outate	outeaten	多吃
outgrow	outgrew	outgrown	生长快
overcome	overcame	overcome	克服
overdo	overdid	overdone	做得过分
overdraw	overdrew	overdrawn	透支
overgrow	overgrew	overgrown	过度生长
oversleep	overslept	overslept	睡过头
overtake	overtook	overtaken	追上
overthrow	overthrew	overthrown	推倒
pay	paid	paid	付出
prove	proved	proved	证明
put	put	put	放
quit	quitted, quit	quitted, quit	退出
read	read	read	读
rebuild	rebuilt	rebuilt	重建
relay	relaid	relaid	转送
repay	repaid	repaid	报答
retell	retold	retold	重述
rid	rid	rid	除去
ride	rode	ridden	骑
ring	rang	rung	响
rise	rose	risen	升起
run	ran	run	跑
saw	sawed	sawn, sawed	锯
say	said	said	说
see	saw	seen	看见
seek	sough	sough	搜索
sell	sold	sold	卖
send	sent	sent	送

Infinitive	Past Tense	Past Participle	Explanation
set	set	set	设置
sew	sewed	sewn, sewed	缝补
shake	shook	shaken	摇晃
shall	should	—	将
shave	shaved	shaved, shaven	剃须
shine	shone, shined	shone, shined	照耀
shoot	shot	shot	射击
show	showed	shone, showed	展示
shrink	shrank, shrunk	shrank, shrunk	萎缩
shut	shut	shut	关闭
sing	sang	sung	唱歌
sink	sank, sunk	sunk, sunken	下沉
sit	sat	sat	坐
sleep	slept	slept	睡觉
smell	smelt, smelled	smelt, smelled	闻
speak	spoke	spoken	讲话
speed	sped, speeded	sped, speeded	促进
spell	spelt, spelled	spelt, spelled	拼写
spend	spent	spent	花钱
spin	spun	spun	旋转
spit	spat, spit	spat, spit	吐
split	split	split	劈开
spoil	spoilt, spoiled	spoilt, spoiled	破坏
spread	spread	spread	散布
spring	sprang, sprung	sprung	弹跳
stand	stood	stood	站立
steal	stole	stolen	偷窃
stick	stuck	stuck	粘贴
strike	struck	struck, stricken	打动
string	strung	strung	捆扎
strive	strove, strived	striven, strived	奋斗
swear	swore	sworn	发誓
sweep	swept	swept	打扫
swim	swam	swum	游泳
swing	swung	swung	摆动
take	took	taken	拿到

Appendix B Irregular Verbs

Infinitive	Past Tense	Past Participle	Explanation
teach	taught	taught	教
tear	tore	torn	撕
tell	told	told	讲述
think	thought	thought	思考
throw	threw	thrown	投掷
underdo	underdid	underdone	不尽力
understand	understood	understood	理解
undertake	undertook	undertaken	担任
unwind	unwound	unwound	打开
upbuild	upbuilt	upbuilt	在上面建
uprise	uprose	uprisen	起义
upset	upset	upset	颠覆
upsweep	upswept	upswept	向上弯曲
wake	waked, woke	waked, woken, woke	醒来
wear	wore	worn	穿着
weave	wove	woven	编织
weep	wept	wept	哭泣
wet	wetted, wet	wetted, wet	打湿
win	won	won	获胜
wind	winded, wound	winded, wound	缠绕
withdraw	withdrew	withdrawn	撤退
work	worked	worked	工作
write	wrote	written	写

References

[1] 王文杰,李金娥,侯依娜. 英语 基础模块 第1册[M]. 北京:北京邮电大学出版社,2016.

[2] 郑淑媛. 英语(基础模块)练习册 第二册[M]. 北京:北京出版社,2011.

[3] 杨亚军. 英语 第一册[M]. 2版. 北京:北京出版社,2019.

[4] 何艳红,吴波,贺娟. 英语语法[M]. 北京:中央民族大学出版社,2015.

[5] 万珍妮,傅瑶. 高职基础英语综合教程[M]. 北京:国家行政学院出版社,2019.

[6] 张前蓉. 全国高等学校英语应用能力A级考试指南[M]. 北京:北京理工大学出版社,2018.

[7] 周新云,杨小凤. 新编高职高专英语语法教程(修订版)[M]. 长沙:湖南科学技术出版社,2014.